Looking for Palestine

"The scholar Edward Said was born in Jerusalem when it was Palestine under the British Mandate, immigrated to the United States, was baptized an Episcopalian, supported Palestinian independence, married a Lebanese Quaker, and became a prominent professor at Columbia University. No wonder his daughter, Najla, was conflicted about her identity. If Edward's Orientalism provides the intellectual framework for understanding postcolonialism, Najla's memoir, *Looking for Palestine*, is the other side of the coin, as those same complex forces tug her life in multiple directions while she tries to understand who she is."
　　　　　　　　　　　　　　　　　　　　　　　—The Daily Beast

"In her engaging memoir, *Looking for Palestine*, Najla Said explores the cultural confusions of growing up Arab-American in the 1970s and '80s New York City."
　　　　　　　　　　　　　　　　　　　　　　　　　　　—Elle

"What proves substantive and memorable about this book . . . is the author's exploration of her relationship with her family and her social surroundings. . . . Her snapshots of personal interaction with her father and their sometimes droll exchanges give the book an undeniably warm and intimate feel."
　　　　　　　　　　　　　　　　　　—San Francisco Chronicle

"Said's aching memoir explores her coming-of-age as a Christian Arab-American on New York's Upper West Side. . . . [Her] complex persona, self-deprecationg humor, and focus on the personal rather than the political broaden the appeal of Said's book beyond any particular ethnic, cultural, or religious audience."
　　　　　　　　　　　　　—Publishers Weekly (starred review)

"In an illuminating memoir, the daughter of Edward Said, the writer, academic, and symbol of Palestinian self-determination, explores her complex family history and its role in shaping her identity. . . .

An enlightening, warm, timely coming-of-age story exploring the author's search for identity framed within the confounding maze of America's relationship with the Middle East." —*Kirkus Reviews*

"It can be a difficult story to tell: that of one's discontent in the midst of privilege. And yet with great skill, humor, and poignancy, Ms. Said accomplishes just that. In the end, she is her late father's great inheritor, ever-journeying toward that elusive home."

—Alicia Erian, author of *Towelhead*

"Najla Said's *Looking for Palestine* is a compassionate and candid book on her courageous coming-of-age in contemporary America. Said is a brilliant, talented and sensitive artist with a larger-than-life, loving father." —Professor Cornel West

"A deeply penetrating, often hilarious, and occasionally devastating account of growing up Arab-American. Of course, Najla Said's scramble for her identity is uniquely hers. How many of us, after all, have had world-famous intellectuals as fathers, experienced the civil war in Lebanon firsthand, and been kissed on the cheek by Yasir Arafat (which she hated)? But after finally finding the conviction to be at peace with herself, Najla Said has written more than a memoir. *Looking for Palestine* is a survivor's guide for all of us who live with that feeling of being out of place wherever we are."

—Moustafa Bayoumi, author of *How Does It Feel to Be a Problem?: Being Young and Arab in America*

"Thoughtful, searching, and open-eyed, *Looking for Palestine* takes readers on a journey into an Arab-American girl's search for identity. The joy and pain of growing up in the long shadow of a brilliant parent, the struggle for meaning and belonging, and the painful dispossession of the Palestinians are all treated with tender care as Najla Said gives us a haunting and singular life story."

—Diana Abu-Jaber, author of *Crescent*

looking
for palestine

growing up confused
in an arab-american family

NAJLA SAID

RIVERHEAD BOOKS
New York

RIVERHEAD BOOKS
Published by the Penguin Group
Penguin Group (USA) LLC
375 Hudson Street, New York, New York 10014, USA

USA • Canada • UK • Ireland • Australia • New Zealand • India • South Africa • China

penguin.com

A Penguin Random House Company

The Library of Congress has catalogued the Riverhead hardcover edition as follows:

Said, Najla.
Looking for Palestine : growing up confused in an Arab-American
family / Najla Said.
p.   cm.
ISBN 978-1-59448-708-8
1. Said, Najla—Childhood and youth.   2. Arab-Americans—Biography.   3. Arab-
Americans—Ethnic identity.   4. Upper West Side (New York, N.Y.)—Biography.
5. Upper West Side (New York, N.Y.)—Ethnic relations.   6. New York (N.Y.)—
Biography.   7. New York (N.Y.)—Ethnic relations.   8. Said, Edward W.—Family.
9. Fathers and daughters—United States.   I. Title.
E184.A65S24   2013   2013016674
305.892'70730747—dc23

First Riverhead hardcover edition: August 2013
First Riverhead trade paperback edition: September 2014
Riverhead trade paperback ISBN: 978-1-59463-275-4

PRINTED IN THE UNITED STATES OF AMERICA

Cover design by Janet Hansen
Front cover photograph by Edward W. Said
Book design by Katy Riegel

For my parents

looking for
palestine

I am a Palestinian-Lebanese-American Christian woman, but I grew up as a Jew in New York City.

I began my life, however, as a WASP.

I was born in Boston to an Ivy League literature professor and his wife, baptized into the Episcopal Church at the age of one, and, at five, sent to an all-girls private school on the Upper East Side of Manhattan, one that boasts among its alumnae such perfectly formed and well-groomed American blue bloods as the legendary Jacqueline Onassis. It was at that point that I realized that something was seriously wrong—with me.

With my green seersucker tunic, its matching bloomers (worn underneath for gym and dance classes), the white

Peter Pan collar of my blouse, and my wool kneesocks, I was every bit the Chapin schoolgirl. I was proud of my new green blazer with its fancy school emblem and my elegant shoes from France. But even the most elaborate uniform could not protect against my instant awareness of my differences. I was a dark-haired rat in a sea of blond perfection. I didn't live on the Upper East Side, where everyone else in my class seemed to live, but on the Upper *West* Side, or, rather, so far beyond the boundaries of what was then considered the Upper West Side as to be unacceptable to many. I did not have a canopy bed, an uncluttered bedroom, and a perfectly decorated living room the way my classmates did or like the homes I saw on TV. I had books piled high on shelves and tables, pipes, pens, Oriental rugs, painted walls, and strange houseguests. I was surrounded at home not only by some of the Western world's greatest scholars and writers—Noam Chomsky, Lillian Hellman, Norman Mailer, Jacques Derrida, Susan Sontag, Joan Didion—but by the crème de la crème of the Palestinian Resistance.

I know today there are probably lots of children of immigrants growing up similarly confused by the mixed messages of their lives, pertaining to everything from class to culture to standards of beauty. For me, though, growing up the daughter of a Lebanese mother and a prominent Palestinian thinker in New York City in the 1980s and '90s was confusing and unsettling. I constantly questioned everything about who I was and where I fit in the world, constantly judged my own worthiness and compared myself to others, and I struggled desperately to find a way to reconcile the beautiful, comforting, loving world of my home, culture, and family with the supposed "barbaric" and "backward" place and society others perceived it to be. I wondered why I was "an exception" to the rule of what both Arabs and Americans were "supposed" to be like, and why I was stuck in such an uneasy position.

After years of trying desperately to convince people that they didn't really understand me or the place my family came from, I stopped trying, especially since there was never anyone around to make me feel less alone in my assertions. I resigned myself to believing that everything people said about my culture was true, because it was exhausting and futile to try to convince anyone otherwise. Strangely, though, I also held on tightly to what I knew to be accurate and real about my family and culture. My parents and extended family are entirely responsible for that. I spent years simultaneously pushing them away and drawing them close, until I found a place where I could exist together with them and completely apart from them. Letting go of the idea that I had to have one identity, one way to describe myself, one "real me" hasn't left me any less confused about who I am, but it has certainly left me inspired, engaged, interested, complicated, and aware. And I'd rather be all of those things than just plain old "American," or plain old "Arab."

WITH THE EXCEPTION of my birth in Boston and a year-and-a-half-ish stint in Palo Alto, and then Southern California, I spent the first thirteen years of my life in an apartment building on Morningside Drive between West 119th and 120th streets. My father was a "teacher of English and Comparative Lit-er-a-ture at Columbia University." I learned to pronounce that impressive-sounding title at the age of four, though I had no idea what it meant. When people asked me what my daddy's job was, I'd wrap my brain and articulators around the phrase with great effort and draw it out.

I did recognize the word "Columbia," and I knew what that was (the park where we played after school and on weekends). I also knew that he did something in an office in that campus-park.

To very smart people who study a lot, Edward Said is the "father of postcolonial studies" or, as he told me once when he insisted I was wasting my college education by taking a course on postmodernism and I told him he didn't even know what it was:

"Know what it *is*, Najla? I *invented it*!!!"

I still don't know if he was joking or serious.

To others, he is the author of *Orientalism*, the book that everyone reads at some point in college, whether in history, politics, Buddhism, or literature class. He wrote it when I was four.

As he explained once, when I pressed him to put it into simple English: "The basic concept, is that . . . historically, through literature and art, the 'East,' as seen through a Western lens, becomes distorted and degraded so that anything 'other' than what we Westerners recognize as familiar is not just exotic, mysterious, and sensual but also inherently inferior."

You know, like Aladdin.

It's mainly because of my father that people now say "Asian American" instead of "Oriental."

To *other* people, he is the symbol of Palestinian self-determination, a champion of human rights, equality, and social justice. A "humanist" who "spoke truth to power."

And then still other people insist he was a terrorist, though anyone who knew him knows that's kind of like calling Gandhi a terrorist.

To me, he was my daddy, a dapper man in three-piece suits tailor-made in London. A cute old guy who yelled at me passionately in his weird sometimes British, sometimes American accent and then (five minutes later) forgot he had been upset; the one who brought me presents from all over the world, talked to me about *Jane Eyre*—my favorite book when I was twelve—and held me when I cried. He played tennis and squash, drove a Volvo, smoked a pipe, and collected pens. He was a professor. He was my father.

I always considered myself a "daddy's girl," and he would have agreed. Daddy and I were temperamental soul mates: artistic, dramatic, needy, sensitive, and completely inept at mundane tasks such as paying bills or even opening them. But as a child, I was in fact completely awed by and maybe even scared of Daddy. I have really strong memories of being petrified when the door of his study was closed and I would hear the furious click-clack-*ding* of his IBM typewriter. Maybe I sensed that he was writing, as Nissim Rejwan in *The Jerusalem Post* put it, *"an important book [that was] bound to usher in a new epoch in the world's attitude toward Oriental studies and Oriental scholarship,"* but all I knew was that, when he was in there, I was afraid. And when he emerged, there would be a moment of apprehension; I'd feel out his mood, and usually, if I was lucky, he'd shower me with love and praise in his uniquely expressive and melodic voice.

My mother is the beautiful, kind woman who took care of me. She was born in Beirut, Lebanon, and came from an enormous, loving, and prestigious family. She was the constant, steady presence in my childhood, and knew how to play, sew, draw, cook, clean, drive, bathe, and love my brother and me. Even my dad was kind of dysfunctional without her. In fact, their whole dynamic can be neatly summarized in the story of their wedding day:

On December 15, 1970, my father woke up in his apartment in New York, assessed the weather (an enormous blizzard was descending on the city), and said to my mother, who was living with him, I suppose: "Mariam! Let's go to City Hall and get married." They had, of course, discussed this plan before, but had not set a date or negotiated the specifics. Regardless, upon taking in the heavy swirls of snow, my father knew at once that today was the right day for their nuptials. He theorized that if they left early enough to avoid getting stuck in it, they would actually be able to take advantage of the inclement weather and get the whole wedding procedure done quickly and painlessly, without waiting in long lines or making too big a deal of it.

They arrived downtown, with a witness, by nine a.m. They noticed a large sign over the man-in-charge's head emblazoned with the phrase "No Smoking." This same man-in-charge was smoking an enormous cigar as he leisurely read the newspaper. Next to the "No Smoking" sign was another equally menacing one that said: "Women Who Want to Get Married Have to Be Wearing a Dress" (surely phrased more concisely; I tell the story the way I heard it from my mother). My parents walked in and told the cigar-smoking clerk their intention, and he, without lifting his eyes from the paper he was reading, casually extended the pointer finger of his free hand up toward the second of the two signs—the one about dresses.

My mother, you see, was wearing pants, because it was freezing.

My father "became impatient" (my mother's words). You could practically see the steam coming out of his ears and the rage boiling in his stomach (my words; I wasn't there but I have a pretty good idea that this is what happened). He took a deep breath, laughed condescendingly, and then pointed out to the clerk that *he* was in fact *smoking* under a "No Smoking" sign, and that detail in itself did not give much value to the rule he was attempting to enforce. Unfortunately, my father's tactic did not work. The clerk kept on reading and smoking. His tone growing more anxious by the second, my father persisted in his argument, asserting that they had come all the way down to City Hall from Columbia University on the subway! In a blizzard! The least this man could do was marry them! The clerk did not respond. My father then began to quote a famous literary text (let's say John Stuart Mill's *On Liberty* because my mom can't remember exactly which, and it works), lecturing the clerk on how man makes rules and they come not from God but society and therefore can be broken. My mother nudged my father and said to him urgently but not too forcefully, as is her way, "Edward. Hold on. Hold on. I am going to the bathroom." He looked at her as if she were crazy for announcing her intention in the middle of his speech, but nodded quickly, and then resumed his impassioned sermon on liberty.

My mother disappeared into the bathroom only to emerge five minutes later with her pants removed. Her turtleneck sweater was long enough to cover the upper part of her thighs, and so was the crocheted vest she wore, which her favorite aunt, Najla, had made for her. Since it was freezing, she had worn thick tights underneath her pants; she actually looked completely respectable without her trousers.

(When my mother tells the story, she gets very excited at this point, as she explains how she knew her plan would work despite the seemingly obvious fact that she was not *really* wearing a dress: "You see, these were the days of the *mini*!")

Pleased with her grace and still chic practicality, my mother smiled at my father. Nimbly, elegantly, she had solved what just moments before seemed an enormous problem. My mother then politely faced the clerk: "Okay, I am wearing a dress."

My father stared at her, dumbfounded. The clerk finally looked up from his paper. He cast his glance slowly from my mother's head down to her feet, which were housed in stylish beige suede snow boots (my mother loves shoes and takes great care to describe the shoes she was wearing in any story). He put out his cigar, and stood up.

My father's mouth remained open. He was confused; he thought he was a genius. But the thing is, so is my mom.

෨

MY PARENTS MET in New York in 1967. My mother went there for an extended stay. My father was already a professor and had been in the United States for almost twenty years. They met like this (again, according to my mother):

"Your aunt Joyce [my dad's sister] broke her leg. She had been my friend at university. I went to visit her in the hospital. When I walked into the room, your father was sitting in a chair, eating popcorn. He looked at me and said, 'All right, Joyce, your friend is here. That means I can go,' and he left."

When I point out to my mother that this "story" of how they met is rather lacking in romantic detail, she says, "What? I thought he was rude. It is true."

I've asked Joyce to clarify, more than once. But each time her story is slightly different from the last, and each time, without fail, I become fascinated by some tangential part of the story, such as the details of the fabulous dress her mother had the seamstress make for her when she hosted the alleged party at which my parents were brought together (or was it a double date she went on with them and a friend of my dad's?).

When my brother and I were small, my mom, who already had a master's in library science (and therefore would organize the books in my bedroom according to some version of the Dewey Decimal System, utterly confusing me), did not work, but stayed home with us full time. She took us to sports and dance classes, she sewed and knit and knew how to play games and do art projects with me. She took us to museums and parks and events and plays. She helped me with all my homework. She knew everything, it seemed.

My mother was also the most beautiful lady to walk the earth, and when my parents dressed up to go out at night, her glamour and perfection took my breath away. She was perfectly skinny, 115 pounds, I knew, and I was captivated by her beauty and elegance and thinness. She took care of every single practical concern in the household: she paid the bills, organized the budgets, and handled the bank accounts, major purchases, investments, and everything else my father couldn't be bothered with. It worked out very nicely for him, since the mundane concerns of life seemed to cause him much anxiety. It wasn't only that he *didn't like* doing practical, real-life tasks, he basically *couldn't* do them, they frustrated him so. It was always clear to me that my parents' marriage was a partnership in the truest sense: Daddy was left to do his work, and Mommy was left to do everything else. Even when my mother went on to attend business school and pursue an executive career, when her day consisted mainly of reading books and playing with me, I knew very well that she could run the world if she wanted.

And then there was my brother. Wadie Edward Said, named, according to cultural custom, after our paternal grandfather, was three years older than I.

Our personalities were completely different: he was outrageously energetic, friendly, fearless, athletic, and always, always curious. I was quiet, shy, calm, and still. Wadie perpetually had a question that he *needed* answered, and would ask again and again until he got a response that quenched his curiosity, although there are questions that to this day remain unanswered.

In 1987, we went on a family trip to L.A. for Memorial Day weekend. During an otherwise silent car ride from the airport to the hotel, my brother, who had been gazing quietly out the window, turned his attention to the back of my father's head and asked, matter-of-factly, "Daddy, what *is* Los Angeles?"

"Well, Wadie, it's a city, really. That's about it," was the succinct reply from the front.

"No, but I mean, what *is* it?"

"I told you, it's a city."

"Yeah, but you know what I mean, what is it really?"

"What are you asking me? It's a city. What else can I tell you?"

"I know, but you know what I mean, what *is* it?"

This exchange continued along the same lines for a good thirty minutes, and probably ended only because we had to get out of the car. My father, who probably knew perfectly well what kind of metaphysical answer his fifteen-year-old son was looking for, seemed to take a sort of childish pleasure in seeing just how many times Wadie could ask the same question before giving up. He never, ever did.

There were other things Wadie was fascinated with over the years: Albania, Namibia, Cashmere (and then, inevitably, Kashmir), political mechanisms, law, criminal justice, and the historical realities of the Middle East. But he always had an equally balanced passion for the following: sports of all kinds, tennis in particular, heavy metal (only the real deal: Iron Maiden, Black Sabbath, Motörhead, Thin Lizzy, Judas Priest, and a smattering of others—Metallica before approximately 1986, AC/DC but only with the first lead singer), comic books (unlike most boys, he preferred *Conan the Barbarian* to *Captain America*), rap music (but only if it was old-school; the Jungle Brothers was as far into the future as he went), and just about any random line from any random movie or commercial or song that stuck with him.

He could mimic any accent, create the funniest characters from the depths of his wild imagination, and keep all of us laughing for days. I had a face I reserved for him that simultaneously said "You're *so weird*" and "You are the funniest, most original person I have ever encountered, and I love it." Wadie inherited the wild and wonderful charm of my father, the strange peculiarities, and the relentless fascination with whatever struck his fancy, whether it was something utterly mundane ("Do you wanna know how to make your spit land in exactly the right place? I figured it out") or something quite serious (to my cousin who couldn't remember the name of a certain African country she'd heard of: "You must be thinking of Burkina Faso; it was previously called the Republic of Upper Volta, but they just changed it").

As far as I was concerned, Wadie was there to understand the things I could not, or did not, want to understand. He also seemed to me to be the more loved child. We had albums upon albums of photos of his birth and his infancy, but very few of mine. My mother would explain away my concern by saying: "Naji, by the time you were born, cameras weren't *in fashion* anymore." My mother is enamored of the phrase "in fashion," and though I now realize it's just a direct translation of the French *"à la mode"* and not a really strange attempt to make me feel better (how could the joy of my birth have really been eclipsed by a sudden drop in popularity of recreational camera usage?), it still drives me batty. But I was happy to defer to Wadie as the more important one, because I admired him so much. He made sense of the boring, the factual, and the serious for me, allowing me to keep a firm footing in my youthful, protected fantasy world. I am not sure he had a choice in the matter; he was the older, and he was a boy. In my family, these were harsh realities he couldn't have escaped no matter how much he might have wanted to. He did not have the luxury, as I did, of hiding behind the shields of childish ignorance and female preciousness. But perhaps, in the end, this helped him avoid some of the identity issues I stumbled over later.

Because the first question people often ask when a person claims to be from Lebanon is "Are you Christian or Muslim?" and because the answer to that question, when asked about someone in my mom's family, yields an unlikely and confusing answer, I ought to stop and explain a little more about Lebanon and my family's place in it.

A tiny country on the eastern shores of the Mediterranean, modern-day Lebanon was once, along with modern-day Syria and the countries we now know as Jordan, Palestine, and Israel, part of one large country that was known as Greater Syria. At the onset of World War I, the Ottomans held full control over this region. But when they and the other Axis powers lost the war, they were forced to give over control of the area to the victorious Allies. Britain and France divided the region up between themselves, and the area known as Syria became a French mandate. The French further divided this Syria, creating two smaller countries. The first, which they called Le Grand Liban, is present-day Lebanon. It included Mount Lebanon (where most of the religious minorities—Druzes, Christians, Shiites—lived) and the coastal region (where Beirut, Tripoli, and Sidon are). The second of the two countries they created is modern-day Syria.

Since many of the Christians native to Mount Lebanon had been influenced by Western religious missionaries, they had preferred to remain allied with Europe rather than the Arab world, and so they welcomed the creation of their own, separate nation. Thence springs the commonly believed and perpetuated myth that Lebanese Christians are not Arabs. They are. An Arab is a person whose native language is Arabic.

THE MAIN THING to know is that my maternal great-grandfather, taken with the belief system that holds that God is accessible to us all and requires no intermediary, traded Greek Orthodox Christianity for the Quaker sect, and his descendants stuck with it. Though technically

"Lebanese Christians," my mother's father and mother raised their children to be Quaker, and Arab nationalists—making them one of three Quaker families in the whole country, and a clear minority.

The French ruled Lebanon until 1943, and when they finally departed in 1946, they left a big old mess, with eighteen different recognized religious sects within the native population: Maronite Christians (who were Catholics), Sunni Muslims, and Shiites were the most well represented and held the most power, in descending order. Even Judaism was one of the recognized sects (Quaker was not).

Then, in 1948, the state of Israel was founded, and Lebanon, its neighbor to the north, was inundated with Palestinian refugees. The Palestinians were welcomed and given shelter in camps set up for them in Lebanon, but they never became citizens, because no one thought they were there to stay. They had long been a people with a national identity of their own, and, it was assumed, they would eventually be guaranteed a safe return home.

By the time I was born, in 1974, nothing had changed, except the population. The Christians were still in power, the Palestinians were still living in camps, but the Shiite and Sunni communities had grown and wanted better representation in government. In a really, really, really simple way, this conflict was the basis for the civil war that lasted from 1975 to 1990, and turned Beirut into a dangerous, complicated, mad war zone, and shifted its reputation from being "the Paris of the Middle East" to "hell on earth."

Having lived through the long, complicated, and confusing war (which ended with virtually *no* changes to the governmental structure), I am itching to describe the whole thing this way (courtesy of my friend Hind Shoufani):

One morning, everyone started fighting everyone. New parties mushroomed up overnight and fought each other. No one understood the clusterfuck, but decided to kill their neighbors too. Other countries made alliances that almost immediately were reversed. The war criminals of that era are still in power. No one can keep the facts straight, as nothing about the reasoning made any sense. The end.

As the war progressed throughout the '70s and '80s, the Syrians, Israelis, Palestinians, and Americans all got involved. Groups multiplied and alliances shifted constantly. Many of the Christians blamed the Palestinians for everything, especially when the Israelis invaded in 1982 in order to obliterate the PLO, which had set up its headquarters in the very neighborhood in which my grandparents lived. And when the city was divided into "West Beirut" (for Muslims and Palestinians) and "East Beirut" (for Christians), my family members refused to leave their West Beirut home to live in the East with the other Christians; they refused to hate Palestinians, Muslims, and whomever else they were supposed to hate, and they steadfastly held on to their belief that all of us are just human. At the time, it was a beyond courageous and admirable thing to do; to hold their convictions despite the danger it put them in.

When I was starting to put together the facts about the civil war in my teenage years, I really wanted my family members to be on one side or another so that everything would make sense. I just wanted them to be one of the Christian families that spoke French and followed a certain party logic. I needed to put them in a box, so I could figure out who I was, but then I was told they'd never do that because they didn't hate Palestinians. I found this detail annoying.

❧

AND MEANWHILE, I also knew that I was Palestinian.

❧

MY FATHER was born in Jerusalem in 1935 to a wealthy Palestinian businessman and his much younger, half-Lebanese, half-Palestinian wife. My paternal *jiddo* (Arabic for "grandfather"), Wadie Ibrahim Said, had come to live in

America in 1911, when he was about sixteen years old. He had left his family in Palestine and traveled to the States alone, so as to avoid conscription in the Ottoman army. He stayed in America ten years or so, and became a U.S. citizen. He then returned to Palestine at the request of his mother, and remained there until the creation of the state of Israel, at which point he permanently moved his family to Cairo, where they had another home. (The family was in Cairo when war broke out in Palestine in 1947, and were unable to return when it became Israel, in 1948.) Finally, at the end of his life, he and my grandmother moved to Lebanon, where he died, in 1971. Jiddo Wadie, born into a Protestant family, was baptized into the Anglican Church and attended British schools in Palestine. When he went to America, he became an Episcopalian (which is the same thing as Anglican, really; it's the American version), and so my father and his four sisters were born with American passports, baptized Episcopalian, and raised in Jerusalem and Cairo. Most of them received their college and advanced degrees in the United States. My father actually came to America at fourteen, to attend a prestigious boarding school in Massachusetts, after he had been summarily discharged from the authoritarian British school he went to in Cairo for some apparently irredeemable mischief.

My dad's mom, my *teta* (Arabic for "grandmother") Hilda, was born in Nazareth, Palestine, in 1914. Her father, my great-grandfather Shukri, was, like his future son-in-law Wadie, born a Protestant, and he too had come to America as a young man. He had initially left Palestine for the U.S. in order to pursue a promising business lead, but he somehow ended up in Waco, Texas, where he chose another path altogether: he was ordained a minister in the Baptist Church. So, to reiterate: Shukri Moussa, my Palestinian great-grandfather, who hailed from Nazareth, Palestine, the childhood home of Jesus Christ himself, came to the United States of America to become a minister in a Christian church. He then returned to Nazareth, Palestine (again, the childhood home of Jesus Christ), and established the first Baptist church in Nazareth. Thus, Teta Hilda was brought up in Palestine as an evangelical Christian. She too attended American schools, but left university early in order to marry my grandfather when she was nineteen and he was forty.

Whether it was my parents' intention or not, I was ultimately raised as a Quaker should be. Both of them were secular humanists; they constantly pressed upon my brother and me that all people are the same, and encouraged us to look inside our own selves to figure out what might be the right thing to do in any situation. They never associated themselves or this behavior with any group or religious sect, though. They just lived their lives that way.

When my brother was three years old and I was nine months, we were baptized into the Episcopal Church together. I only recently wondered why we had been baptized at all. My cousin was planning her wedding to a Catholic man, and they were having trouble finding someone to marry them, given their religious differences. My cousin said something about it being all the more complicated because she had not been baptized. I asked her why she hadn't been, and my mom piped in: "Quakers don't baptize."

"Really? Then why were we baptized?"

"Because your grandmother insisted."

"What?"

"Your father's mother, your Teta Hilda. She insisted. I agreed so she wouldn't get upset. It was only water on your head, so I didn't mind. It wasn't something *traumatic*, so I didn't get in an argument about it. Neither your father nor I cared about it."

My mother's disdain for all aspects of organized religion has never been kept a secret from me or from anyone she meets. It is obviously partly because she is Lebanese, and saw her country and its neighbors devastated by religious strife, but I was still disappointed to learn the real, rather ordinary facts behind a part of my identity that I had romanticized.

As a little girl, I had desperately wanted my parents to believe in *something*, *anything*, the way "other people" seemed to, but every time I tried to latch on to a part of my identity, my parents would take it away from me. They always had to make sure that I knew I wasn't *only* Palestinian, or *only* Lebanese, or *only* American. My parents were always *themselves*, whether it was in the context of political parties ("We vote Independent," they'd both insist when I asked whether they were Democrats or Republicans), countries ("We are Arab. Not one *Lebanese* and one *Palestinian*"), or even neighborhoods ("We live in Morningside Heights, which is not *really* the Upper West Side, Najla . . . No, it's not really Harlem either . . . "), so I suppose I had somehow always taken comfort in knowing I was baptized into a specific church, that I "officially" belonged to at least one group in society. Now my mother's story had taken that away too.

My parents further confused me by constantly asserting their Arab-ness, which at the time and in the place I was growing up seemed to be the one thing they ought to be keeping quiet about. My father was always proudly telling everyone he was both Palestinian *and* Arab. I didn't understand why he had to complicate things; his religion was Christian, his expertise not in the field of politics or history; he didn't *have* to make a big deal of it. He was a British/American-educated professor of English and Comparative Literature at Columbia University. He was a literary critic, a philosopher, a teacher, a classical musician, and a thinker. And what he thought about mostly were the books and works of art of "white" people. He had also left the Middle East at the age of fourteen, never to return as anything more than a visitor, so his childhood memories of Palestine, Egypt, and Lebanon, where he had spent most of his time, were of idyllic places where Arab Muslims, Arab Christians, and yes, Arab Jews, lived in a "melting pot" much like the New York City in which I was raised.

∽

AT MY NURSERY SCHOOL, a progressive one for the children of professors and students at Columbia University, there were plenty of international boys and girls with names that were more unheard-of than my own. One quiet Asian girl in my class was named Ai, which was meant to be pronounced like the letter ("I"), or the organ with which a person sees the world ("eye"), but according to me, the name she was given was "spelled wrong" and "not a real name, probably because her parents aren't from America."

I vaguely knew that my parents weren't really from America either, but I didn't feel in any way different from the kids around me. Unlike Ai's parents, who struggled to communicate with the teachers, mine spoke perfect English. It didn't seem odd to me to have parents who spoke a second language—for the most part, every one of the kids who lived in my neighborhood had at least one parent from another country and/or one parent who was a professor. Maybe what seemed so odd to me about Ai's family was that they were *so* foreign, and from only one country. The Woods, our closest friends in the building, were English and Mexican. Michael, the dad, was from England, and had glasses and cardigans and books and a study, just as my dad did. They both taught English and they were great friends. Elena, his wife, was from Mexico. She and my mom were good friends too, and though they both had dark complexions and jet-black hair, they both spoke an English that clearly had been taught to them by British people (they'd say "this bloody thing" and "perhaps" and "jography"). Michael and Elena had three children: Gaby, who was the same age as Wadie; Patrick, who was the same age as me; and little Tony, who was smaller than all of us. The Smits, who lived across the hall from us and also had children who were our age, had a glamorous blond American mother who ran the marathon every year, and a dad who was Dutch and taught history at Columbia. They too were a family much like ours—American, but somehow slightly removed from being fully so. Even our family friends who were "only" American, like the Rosenthals, the Coles, and the Stades, fit perfectly into our world. They might not have been born speaking French, Spanish, or Arabic at home, but I always somehow knew that if they felt like it, they probably could; they, like all of us, were part of the Columbia world, and we were all different, but mostly the same.

But my one "real American" friend, Catherine, seemed as foreign as Ai. Catherine was the only girl in my building whose dad, Jack, wasn't a professor at Columbia. He was the super, and they lived in the basement. He didn't have a study like my dad and Michael Wood did. He had a "shop" with tools and fun stuff that we were sometimes allowed to play with. Catherine's mother, Carol, was an artist, which I thought was the most magnificent thing in the world. She would always embark on projects with us; we once built an entire mini town, partly in the shop with Jack and partly in the apartment with Carol. I vividly remember watching in awe as Carol painstakingly and precisely painted each of the stones on our "church" in a shade of gray, and then out-lined their edges with a darker shade, creating what looked to me like a three-dimensional image. I had never seen any-one do that.

Unlike mine, Catherine's parents never said "the Amer-icans" when they talked about Americans, and they only spoke one language. Catherine's grandmother lived in New Jersey and didn't have to take a plane to visit. Catherine and her parents listened to country music instead of Beethoven, and they didn't seem to wear a lot of itchy wool things. They ate their salad from a separate bowl and got their dressing from a bottle, and they had better snacks in their house than we did in ours. "Real Americans" like Catherine's family were what was completely foreign to me.

Catherine and I used to play that I was Jack LaLanne's daughter, our building was my mansion, our bikes were my horses, and she was my assistant-friend. That was my favorite game. Jack LaLanne seemed like the richest, most famous guy ever, since he was always on TV. He might as well have been the king of America. So, naturally, I wanted to be his little princess. I was sure that, like everyone on TV, Jack LaLanne lived in California, where the sun always shone. I was also sure that he had a wife, who, like everyone in California, had yellow hair and red lips and blue eye shadow, and that he had a gorgeous, perfect, blond daughter, who was me.

Of course, I thought my real, brunette mother was beautiful and perfect, but in a different way. And anyway, on TV and in my books, and according to my many Barbies, the most beautiful people and the princesses were always blond. Real people, boring people, and evil people were brunettes. Blondes were not real people; they were fantasy people, TV people.

My first visit to Lebanon, I was just three weeks old. My second was the following summer, 1975. My brother and I apparently had a wonderful, magical time, while the adults' enjoyment was tainted by the political violence that was brewing. Skirmishes and gunfights had begun around the country in April, and though they were still few and far between, most people knew that something bigger and more dangerous was on the horizon. Certainly no one knew that a fifteen-and-a-half-year civil war was about to rip the country to pieces, but everyone who was old enough to understand it could feel the tension in the air. On a sunny day in early September, Jiddo Emile, my mother's father, drove us to the airport. The streets were eerily quiet. He looked at my parents and said softly, "I think it is good you're leaving now. I have a bad feeling about what is going to happen here." By the time we reached Brussels a few hours later, the Beirut airport had closed; no one was allowed in or out of the country. We didn't go to Beirut the following summer; it wasn't safe. We returned again in January of 1977.

In June of 1978, we set off for what was to be my fifth trip to Lebanon, but we never actually got there. The fighting had gotten so bad by the time we reached London that we ended up staying in the UK for two extra weeks. I had a marvelous time playing at the home of our friends from New York, the Rosenthals, who were living there for a while, and I ran around the garden of my aunt Rosemary's house in Brighton, England, with a smile on my face and a skip in my step. I didn't know we were stranded. I thought Brighton was where we had planned to be.

The memories I have of traveling to and from Lebanon in my first eight years are, for the most part, a big, jumbled collection of delightful images. I adored "Beirut," as the whole country was known to me, and I adored the days we spent there. Remarkably, though the war and I basically came into the world at the same time, and though its presence did make itself known in ways I most certainly did register, it was never part of my primary experience of the country. Perhaps I was too young to understand, and thus too young to be scared. To me, Beirut was love and grandparents.

On the way, we would usually stop in Paris or London, where Wadie's and my main pastime seemed to be getting as much chocolate into our mouths in one day as was humanly possible. There was *pain au chocolat* and Nutella in the morning, *chocolat chaud*, *crème glacée au chocolat*, and just plain old bars of *chocolat* too (I don't know that I was fully aware that these all existed in America as well, as we were never really allowed to have them at home). We would also often visit my aunt Rosemary and her husband, Tony, and I would marvel at my aunt's British-accented speech and perfect manners, and become anxious at her insistence on quizzing Wadie and me on kings named Charles and James and James and Charles. I let Wadie answer for both of us. We were barely old enough to read, but Wadie seemed to have been born with a sophisticated understanding of the whole world and how it fit together that I lacked.

Once in Beirut, we would eat even more chocolate. Wadie would lead me expertly through the streets of Beirut, and clutching his hand, I would maneuver my little body around army tanks, trying not to touch them because they were so hot from the sun they burned my skin. It never occurred to me to wonder why there were tanks in the street, I just knew that I didn't like to touch them.

We'd marvel at our favorite supermarket in the Hamra Street area of Ras Beirut, where we lived. Smith's was stocked from floor to ceiling with every type of food from everywhere in the world; not only did they have Frosted Flakes from America, they also had Frosties from England. Wadie and I knew they were the same but would still try to trick my mom into buying us one box of each. We'd then compare the boxes and make fun of the way they had to change the name of the cereal so the British kids could "understand" it.

We would go to Jiddo Emile's house in Brummana, in the mountains above Beirut, where my mother had spent much of her childhood. There were pine logs on the ceiling in the main room and there was Salimee, the cook, who scared me with her blindness, deafness, and deformed fingers. I never went into the kitchen because of her. I would wait for her to poke her head out and tell us to come eat. I don't remember ever seeing more than her head and torso, in fact, but that was more than enough of her. Salimee was, I later found out, my grandfather Emile's cousin. She had contracted typhus as a child, which left her disabled and, later, uneducated and unmarried. My grandfather wanted to help, so he hired her to cook for the family. It was a very nice thing to do, though it didn't make her less scary to me.

In Brummana we would play in the trees and sometimes in the mud. We would help light bonfires made out of pine needles, and we'd sit outside on wicker stools when we ate our dinner. We would play with our many, many cousins, all of whom seemed to be older than I was, and with Tony and Rita, who lived in a tiny, one-room house off the side of our own. Their father worked for my grandfather, and although they lived in that tiny room with their parents, the grounds were as much theirs as they were ours. I thought they were part of our family. In so many ways, they were.

When we were down in Beirut we would go to the Golf Club every day to eat hamburgers, French fries, and ice cream bars, practice our swimming strokes and complicated dives, and run around with my three first cousins on my dad's side: Saree, Ussama, and Karim. I thought that that's how families were supposed to be: big and boundless and all-encompassing. I thought that once two people got married, their separate families would become one big one, everyone would live on the same street, and all the kids would be friends and cousins. The Makdisi boys have always felt more to me like three extra, loving, taunting, wonderful big brothers than cousins who lived five thousand miles away. It seemed like wherever I went in Lebanon, all my grandparents and all my cousins, aunts, and uncles were there too. It was fantastic.

In the summer of 1979, when I was five years old, we went to Spain before Lebanon. Since I was five, I had no idea that our trip to Toledo, Seville, Córdoba, Granada,

Torremolinos, and Málaga was a trip through Andalusia. Had I been fifteen, I might have rolled my eyes and complained about the stupidity and weird exclusivity of "seeing only the *Arab* part of Spain," but since I wasn't fifteen, I had a tremendous time.

We flew from Málaga to Beirut. It was our first time there since Teta Wadad, my mother's mother, had died. I worried that Mommy would be sad. I held her hand. I was so happy to see Jiddo Emile and to be back in my favorite place. I loved to sit with him at the dining room table every morning and watch him peel a hard-boiled egg and then mash it into his *labne*, strained yogurt, with *za'atar* and *zeit*, thyme and olive oil. I'd eat my Frosties and ask him questions about the chickens on the roof of the building next door. We lived in a modern building on a modern street, but for some reason there was an old house across the street with chickens and lambs and pigeons on the roof. I was enchanted by this bizarre view into the home of our neighbors, who seemed to live in a storybook. I loved that Beirut seemed so much like New York most of the time, but that every so often I would notice something magical about the place, like farm animals on roofs, or houses with big gates and enormous trees right next to a hotel or a supermarket. Everyone in Beirut had a balcony off each room (Teta Hilda called them "verandas"). I wished we had one in New York.

We had only fire escapes, and the only people who ever used them, according to Nick, our elevator man, were robbers.

ↄ⅁

WE WENT TO THE GOLF CLUB a lot that summer. My aunt Grace, who was young and cool and wore a gold anklet on her teeny tanned ankle, would sometimes pick Wadie and me up in her little Volkswagen Bug and drive us down the Corniche to the Golf Club. I would stare up at the palm trees that lined the Mediterranean as she drove through the mad traffic, and I'd try to memorize the words to the songs on the radio. I wondered why the lady who sang that one song I kept hearing ("I will survive!") was so mad at her boyfriend (I had somehow been able to figure out that she wasn't hoping to survive a fire or cancer), but I didn't want to ask Grace. I made up my own story as we sped along. I would act it out later, in the bathtub, using the *douche téléphone* as my mic.

There was no beach at the Golf Club, just a big pool and lots of places to lounge around. There was a snack bar that had good ice cream and even better French fries. There must have been a golf course somewhere, but I never saw it. No one I knew played golf anyway. Wadie would play with Karim, Ussama, Saree, and their friends, and I would play by myself. Every so often one of my cousins would play with me for a minute, but mostly they just teased me. *"Naji Baji, pudding and pie, kissed the boys and made them cry,"* they would whine again and again, mockingly. But I liked the attention. I was the only girl, and the littlest one, and I was thrilled to be noticed.

One afternoon we heard shooting in the distance. The lifeguards blew their whistles and told our parents to take us into the changing rooms; the fighting was very close. I have no recollection of being afraid or even knowing why we had to go hide in the changing rooms. I thought we were taking a break from the pool; I knew you weren't supposed to swim if you'd just eaten. When the danger passed, we returned to the pool and splashed around for the rest of the day. Saree dove down into the pool and came up with bullets. We made a pile of them on the side of the pool, next to the filter thing. When it was time to go, I gathered up my towel and went back to the ladies' changing room with Mommy and Grace. Mommy and I showered together, and then dressed side by side in front of the locker we shared. It took me about three minutes to change back to my T-shirt, shorts, and clogs. Mommy combed and fixed my hair quickly, and when I complained that my barrettes didn't match, Mommy said, "It's okay, it's *the fashion* to wear two different barrettes," to shut me up.

I rolled my bathing suit up into my towel as she had

taught me, and I put the little bundle into my new bag from Spain. It was red and made of cloth, and there was an ice cream cone embroidered on the front of it. I loved having my own bag. Within about ten minutes, I had gone into and come out of the changing room. I didn't understand why it always took everyone else what seemed like two hours.

I walked in circles around the area in front of the changing rooms, singing to myself. I clambered up and down the huge stone stairway that led to the pool area. And then I slipped and fell down the stairs, somehow twisting my right thumb, banging it against the heavy stone, and ultimately landing with all my weight on top of it.

When we arrived back home, Teta Hilda took one look at my purple, swollen thumb and insisted it was broken, which led my mother and me to the American University hospital, five blocks away. We were walking in the emergency entrance when a car stopped in front of us. The door opened and a young man and woman came out of the back with an older woman between them. Each of the young people held on to one side of the older woman's body as they guided her toward the hospital door, and the man held a blood-soaked cloth to the side of her head. She was wailing and he was trying to console her. My eyes widened and Mommy clutched me closer. I could tell from her reaction that this was a really bad thing that I probably shouldn't see. When I asked my mother what had happened to the woman, she said, "I don't know exactly, but I know she will be okay, Naji. She got hit in the head somehow. Don't worry. They will fix her." I knew enough to know that a gun or bomb was involved, that she hadn't just bumped into a cabinet. Even after my mother turned my body away from the sight of her, I twisted my head around to stare fixedly at the woman as she was guided to the elevator, still shrieking, now invoking God. I remember feeling mostly sad for her son and daughter. They were grown-ups but they looked very scared.

That fall I returned to New York, and to a world that could not have been more different. I was starting kindergarten at the Chapin School for girls, on East End Avenue, between 84th and 85th streets.

Because my father was a professor, and because almost everyone in my mom's family was an educator as well, it was important to my parents that my brother and I receive the best education possible. In the 1970s, when I started school, the public schools in the neighborhood where we lived were not up to my parents' standards. In addition, Teta Wadad had been the headmistress of an all-girls school in Beirut for forty years. My mom attended her mother's school, Aliah (which was the first and only secular, national school in the country), and had a wonderful experience there, so she thought I might have a similar one if I attended an all-girls private school in New York. And so I was sent to Chapin.

Chapin is on the Upper East Side of Manhattan, just two blocks away from an equally prestigious girls' school, Brearley, to which I had not been admitted, probably because I had failed to say a single word during my admissions interview. To me, the only discernible difference between the two schools was the color of their uniforms (blue for Brearley, green or yellow for Chapin). But owing partly to the schools' distinct reputations ("intellectual girls" went to Brearley, "society girls" to Chapin) there were more girls in my Columbia community who went to Brearley. And since both were across town (too far to walk), I would carpool with the Brearley girls from my neighborhood.

It didn't take me long to see all the ways in which I was different from my Chapin classmates, who seemed to live very close together. Not only did I live very far away from them, but their homes were much fancier.

In first grade, when most of us started riding school buses, we were divided further by neighborhood. There were two "official" Chapin buses, and a separate one for "the West Siders." The "official" buses were great big green chartered buses, one for "Uptown" (which I think still went only as far north as 96th Street), and one for "Downtown" (which got to about 62nd Street). Early social connections were formed around where you lived and, consequently, which bus you were on. Every morning and afternoon, the two grand green coaches would be parked in front of school, and young Chapin girls in green and yellow pinafores would clamber out of and into their enormous and, to me, elegant doors. There didn't even seem to be anyone actually driving these buses, and I was certain that if they were not driven by robots, their mysterious, hidden drivers were jolly old white-uniformed men who looked like Sam the butcher on *The Brady Bunch*.

The school bus that I was on, however—the "West Side Bus"—was not big and fancy and did not even belong to Chapin like the others did; it was owned and operated by a private company. It was small, dirty, and yellow.

New York was a very different city when I was growing up from what it is now. In general, families with money lived on the Upper East Side, or they aspired to. There were wealthy families in other parts of the city too, of course, but class lines were much more strictly recognized and kept. The city was not all gentrified; there was a lot of crime. Parts of downtown Manhattan were lovely, but parts were still very dangerous, and the same was true of the Upper West Side. Parents who raised their kids downtown were generally in the arts, and the ones who raised their kids on the Upper West Side were generally more liberal, more intellectual, and more Jewish. Most of my East Side friends' parents had gone to Ivy League schools and were very successful at what they did, but what they did usually involved Wall Street firms and large corporations. There were few pockets of the city that were completely safe, but even though a kid could get robbed on the Upper East Side just as easily as anywhere else, for the most part it was the safe place to raise your kids, if you could afford to live there.

Across Central Park (a den of crooks and drug addicts and thieves if you went to the wrong part at the wrong time and without a grown-up) was the Upper West Side, which had many more run-down sections then. At its highest end, the Upper West Side turned into Harlem, a place that was still almost entirely African American. Everything about the city was more segregated at the time, and for the most part, we all stayed where we lived and felt we belonged.

Between the Upper West Side and Harlem, there is a little neighborhood that spans about fifteen blocks north to south (from 110th Street to 125th Street), and maybe four blocks east to west. This neighborhood is where Columbia University sits, and it is where I grew up.

It was clear to me that none of the kids in my building were allowed to walk farther uptown than our street—

120th—without a grown-up (not that the grown-ups ever went that far uptown, either) and that the kids who did live a block or two farther up mostly went to public school and their parents weren't affiliated with Columbia. I didn't need to be well versed in social stratification to figure out that among families I lived near, mine was one of the "fancier" ones, but among the ones at my school, mine was one of the shabbier ones. It was all pretty well laid out for me by geography.

I began to keep a running list in my head of everything about me that seemed even the littlest bit different from others at school. Some of my classmates had one parent who spoke another language, but I was pretty sure I was the only one who had two. If one of my friends asked an innocent question like "What street do you live on?" I would recoil in shame. I lived on "Morningside Drive." My address didn't sound at all like anyone else's; there was neither a specific street number on which my building sat (for example, 65th) nor an avenue location for it (Park, Madison, Second, Third, and so on) that any of my friends had ever heard of. I loved my building and my neighborhood friends but I didn't understand why none of them were at my school. Was I being sent to Chapin as a punishment? I didn't understand why I was put into a place where I might not really belong. I loved reading and learning and didn't so much mind being there during the day, but I became consumed with cataloging only what was different about me. Slowly I began to think of little else, day in and day out. It became a compulsion: Why do Ashley and Katie have the same headband and I don't? Why does everyone have a dog or a cat and I have chameleons? Why doesn't anyone know what hummus is? Why do I have Arabic bread? Why is my brother's name weird? Why is *my* name weird? I started to dread going to school. I felt like a complete freak.

Because I was the first one on my small school bus to be picked up every morning—because I lived farthest away—I woke in the darkness of the early dawn and rode alone on the bus with Frank the driver, who called me "Snots-a-lot." Many English speakers have trouble with the "j" and "l" right next to each other in my name's spelling, and will add an extra syllable, making my name "Nadj-uh-luh." (Italians add this syllable too, but I don't mind it because it sounds like they're speaking Italian.) Frank was one of many people who thought my name was pronounced "Nadj-uh-luh" and, unfortunately, he decided that "Nadj-uh-luh" rhymed with "Snots-a-lot." Thus, the first of what were to be many derogatory nicknames for me was born. Being with Frank, alone, on that bus, every single morning, all the way from 119th Street to 101st Street (where the next girl got on), I was overcome with loneliness and isolation. My school and the girls who attended it seemed to exist in a different world: a world that woke under the light and warmth of the sun, a world where families sat at the breakfast table together and ate eggs and toast and played with their golden retriever.

My heart ached with envy as I dressed in the cold dark and thought of my classmates, still sleeping peacefully in their canopied beds for another hour or so. From my bedroom window, I could see across Morningside Park to the East Side, and I could watch the sun rise over the other half of the city, where I knew they all lived. Daddy made me a Thomas' English muffin with butter and jam, and gave me a glass of orange juice, and for those few minutes, I always felt safe and happy. But as the clock hands inched closer to seven a.m., a lump would grow in my throat. Fear and loneliness rose from my toes into the pit of my stomach. The thought of being torn away from my parents was unimaginable.

Yet I gathered from the grown-ups around me that I was supposed to be happy. It felt like they were trying to convince me with their eager looks and optimistic waves that Frank was driving me from prison to Candy Land, and I should be grateful and thankful that I was allowed to go. My thoughts began to multiply and grow in horror: What if something happened, and I was stuck at school? What if they divided up the city as they had done in Beirut and I wasn't allowed back to my side? I would be alone forever with people who looked different from me, who didn't hug me, and Mommy and Daddy would be gone.

And then I found out, upon inviting them over to play, that some of my friends were not *allowed* to come to my house unless my parents could guarantee that we would be picked up from school by one of them and taken safely to the door of my apartment in a car or a taxi. That's how egregious they found our Harlem-bordering neighborhood. Likewise, if one of the parents of said friend could not physically come to my house after the playdate in a car or a taxi to pick up their daughter, a playdate *chez moi* was completely out of the question. Babysitters were not allowed to substitute for parents on these occasions. Of course, my mother thought it was all ridiculous, and she scoffed at the offensive restrictions, while I sank into myself, feeling ashamed for even thinking that my house was worth coming over to.

I quickly figured out, based on who invited me to her house, and how friendly her parents were to mine, whom I could risk inviting over, and the number stayed small and exclusive for the entire nine years I attended Chapin. My parents found the whole situation laughable and stupid, and told me that the parents of the girls who weren't allowed at my house were snobs, and I shouldn't want anything to do with them anyway. When I was ten, my father overheard

my friend ask me on the phone if I could find some tumbleweed in my neighborhood for our prairie diorama, and he
roared with laughter for a good hour. How was she supposed to know there wasn't any tumbleweed on Morningside Drive? She'd never been to my house!

That I was from the wrong side of the *global* tracks as well became clearer as the '80s began to unfold, and "Beirut" became synonymous with "war."

As a little Chapin girl in the early 1980s, it was *Lebanese* that I never wanted to be. The "Palestinian" thing never made sense. It was this funny word that my dad would use to describe himself, and I didn't even know it referred to a place. It could have been a dietary practice, a blood type, or a disease. My mother never described herself as a Palestinian, so I did not know that because Daddy was one, I was one too. Frankly, it seemed that as long as I wasn't from behind the Iron Curtain, where it was ice-cold, and where people waited in line for food and spoke like robots, I wasn't a threat. There were also very few Jewish girls in my school, and certainly no Israelis, so my lack of "Arab pride" was not completely unfounded.

And then I gradually came to learn what an Arab was and, consequently, spent a good portion of the rest of my childhood avoiding the fact that I might actually be one. It was 1979 when I began school, and the attacks of September 11 were twenty-two years away, but the words "Arab" and "Muslim" were already synonymous with "crazy, violent terrorists." Palestinians had already hijacked planes and killed Israeli athletes at the Olympics, and Lebanon was on the front page of the paper every day, engulfed in flames and fire. I was both too young to understand and hadn't been schooled in the intricacies of the Lebanese Civil War, the Israeli occupation of Palestinian lands, and the historical context of things, so when my friends made passing comments about Beirut being the most awful, dangerous place on earth, when they asserted that the Lebanese were all violent, machine-gun-wielding lunatics ("except for your family, Najla. But you're really American anyway"), and that Muslims were "weird angry" people, I couldn't really counter them with anything but a silent, sad nod.

And was I really Arab? I didn't understand how I could be. My father, the English professor, spoke Arabic sometimes with my mom and had family in Lebanon but sounded and seemed perfectly American to me. In addition, we were, as

I have explained, Christian—Episcopal Baptist Presbyte-
rian Quakers. Many of the girls I went to school with were
Episcopalians, and I clung joyfully to the fact that I was a
baptized Episcopalian, and dropped that piece of precious
information into whatever conversation I could. For a sensitive young girl acutely aware of her differences, this one tiny
similarity meant an enormous amount. So I didn't go to the
church on the Upper East Side that all my friends went to
(or any church for that matter). The mere fact that *I could
have gone there* was enough to save me from total rejection.

"Are you Jewish or Christian?" became the question of
the month at school.

"Christian," I'd say with relief. I felt terribly sad for the
Jewish girls, who were in the minority, but I was mostly
glad there was a new question to answer, and it was one to
which I had the "right" answer.

THE IRONY IS, I probably knew more about Judaism at
that point than I did about Christianity. As a family, we
celebrated Christmas and Easter, but we never went to
church. My grandparents were more religious than my parents, and in the very progressive time and place in which I
grew up, everyone was trying to make sure that kids heard
different stories and learned about the whole world. By the

time I was five, I knew more African and French songs than English ones, and more about origami, Chinese New Year, and the Children of Israel than I did about myself.

During my first year of nursery school we had had a Hanukkah party one week and a Christmas party the next. At the Hanukkah party, we ate potato latkes on blue tablecloths; we heard the story of Judas Maccabeus and learned the dreidel song. Everyone got a dreidel (I still have mine), and the girls were given fans, and the boys, plastic swords. My friend Noah showed his mom his sword and told her about how "the Jewish people got to fight for their freedom." She told him he was one of those people. He was happy. I was happy for him.

My mom participated happily in Hanukkah day, as she had done for the party we had had for a Japanese holiday earlier in the year. But when she was handed a set of instructions about what was acceptable for the Christmas party, my mother spoke up. She went to my teacher and said, "Look, I don't care a *damn* about religion but if you are going to teach them all about Hanukkah and tell the story of Judas Maccabeus and oil that burned for so many days, why do you have restrictions on what we are allowed to teach them about Christmas?" She pointed to the list and read aloud: "'No angels, no Jesus, no "Hark! The Herald Angels Sing," no stars, no wise men. Reindeer, Santa Claus, bells, trees, and "Frosty the Snowman" are all okay'? How silly. If you are going to tell them one story, you should tell them the other. It's not like they won't need to learn who Jesus was at some point in their lives."

"We don't want to offend the Jewish families," my teacher said.

"Well, what about the Muslim families, and the Hindu families, and the secular families? Do you want to offend *them*?"

Another mother, who was Turkish, piped up: "Yes. You know, we celebrated Ramadan not too long ago, and no one asked us if we'd like to have a party to teach the kids about it."

The next year, the teachers allowed my mother to read us a very smart children's version of the Nativity story that related the story of Jesus's birth in as unreligious a way as possible. At home, though, we never actually mentioned Jesus, much to the chagrin of Teta Hilda. My parents were adamantly secular. To me, Christmas was about presents and giving to the poor, and Easter was about chocolate bunnies and pretty dresses. But I always remember my mom's insistence that we treat everyone equally, even when it came to religion, which she abhorred.

Not only did they all belong to the "right" church, but everyone in my family also spoke English and French along with Arabic, which made us "cosmopolitan" (in my head), and my grandmother wore Chanel suits, played bridge, and visited mud baths in Czechoslovakia. I traveled to Lebanon frequently, and I ate Arabic food at home. But even though my mother spoke to me in Arabic a lot of the time, and knew only the French words for my headbands, stockings, and underwear, I had no idea she spoke with an accent until my friend Caroline told me so when we were in the fourth grade. For the most part, I was wholly unaware of the political realities of the Middle East. I didn't know what Muslims were because as far as I knew I'd never met one. Preschool had introduced me to some Jewish friends, and the candles and the dreidels, but I certainly didn't know what Israel was or what Zionism might be, and if I had known, I surely would not have been able to make a connection between those two things and a menorah.

When Teta Hilda came to kindergarten with me on Grandparents' Day, she looked just as fancy as all the other grandmas and grandpas. I knew she was not "American" in the same way that some of them were, and the way that Catherine's nana from Elizabeth, New Jersey, was, but I also did not know what an Arab was, let alone what one was "supposed" to look like. Teta looked, dressed, and behaved most like the Chapin grandparents who were from France and Sweden and Italy. Her accent, like my dad's, was almost nonexistent, and sounded more fancy than foreign. Her clothes were elegant and ladylike—hardly appropriate for hanging out in a sandbox—and she was very impressed with all that was proper and genteel about Chapin. She knew by heart all the Episcopal hymns that we sang at Morning Prayers, nodded in approval at the manners we were taught, and then took me for tea at the Stanhope Hotel, on Fifth Avenue, at the end of the day. So I assumed that Beirut was probably somewhere in Paris.

But as I grew older and progressed into the first, second, and third grades, a sense of shame about my differences—my hairy arms, my weird name, my family's missing presence on the Social Register—took over my thoughts. My grandmother's once "fancy" accent began to sound simply "foreign."

ও৪

IN A FIRST-GRADE production of *The Frog Prince*, I was cast as the king. I stared sullenly at the Burger King crown and bathrobe that were meant to be my costume. The girls who played the queen and the princess got to wear tiaras and their fancy pink party dresses. One of them was Sarah Pedersen, the only other Middle Eastern girl in my class. You would never have known her mother was from Iran unless you saw her, which I did, for the first time, on Parents' Day in 1980. Sarah's dad was from Norway, and she had been "blessed" with long, beautiful blond hair. She lived on the Upper East Side, and she had a "normal" American name. Her mom, who was quite beautiful, like my own, had dark skin and hair, and an accent. But Sarah looked nothing like her. Couldn't my mother see that I looked wrong? Why hadn't she made the effort to "fix" me?

I knew I'd been cast as the king partly because of my size. I knew exactly how much I weighed and how tall I was, and I also knew exactly how much everyone else weighed and how tall they all were. Every year at Chapin, we would be lined up in alphabetical order and sent down to the nurse's office to be weighed and measured. One by one we'd step up onto the scale, and Mrs. Giusti would call out our weight for whoever was writing it down. Then we'd quickly turn our backs to be measured lengthwise, our height would be called out and registered, and we'd hop off into the huddle of our classmates:

"What's your weight, Najla?"

"Seventy-five."

"Mine's seventy."

"Oh."

A newly weighed and measured girl would inevitably appear at that moment.

"Hey!!! Mine's seventy too!!"

"*Yay!!!* Oh my God!!! We're twins!!!"

One year, I spent the whole bus ride home staring at my thighs. I was mad at them for being so big. How was it that

I was seventy-five pounds and one of my best friends was seventy-four, *and* she was taller than I was?

That's when I figured out what the real difference was between me and the other girls. With my mop of tangled black hair, a deep, husky voice, and a faint mustache, with my far too heavy frame, I was obviously not a girl at all. I was a boy, or at least one gene away from it.

Thus it was in 1980, when I was six years old and in grade one, that my self-esteem began to slip. I became deeply aware of my long arms and legs and began to resent my lanky, undainty form. I had been shy before, and quiet, but I'd had a confidence about myself that was clear. (You can see remarkable evidence of this poise in all my early photos; I look sassy and self-assured, bright and brazen.) Before Chapin, and even perhaps through my first year there, any awareness I had of my body and mind had been positive (I was the tallest! I had the biggest feet and hands! I could read a whole book fast! I could spell anything! I was a really good drawer!). But by the end of first grade, my self-image had been translated into "fat, big, hairy, and weird."

From then on, I made a concerted effort not to stand out at school. I was quiet, and good, and sweet. I did my work and I paid attention as best I could. I was unwaveringly obedient and worked very hard to stay on the teachers' good sides. For the most part, I succeeded. At lunch in lower school, we would sit at long tables and eat together, family-style. Our homeroom teacher would sit at the head and serve us, one by one, the dishes we would politely request, and I always smiled sweetly at the teacher and said quietly, "Everything, please." I said that phrase—"everything, please"—unfailingly, every single day of my lower school tenure. While the other girls would boldly ask for "just mashed potatoes" or "meat loaf and potatoes but no beans" or (most shockingly) "just bread and butter" on any given day, I never once did the same. I actually did not know what I wanted, or liked. I was unfamiliar with the food to a certain degree (we never had macaroni and cheese or meat loaf or grilled cheese or creamed spinach at home), so there was no way I actually knew in advance if I would like it, but I also was very afraid of standing out. I felt it best to be inoffensive and benign, to just ask for it all and eat what I could. Eventually, I became all too aware that I ate "everything" and the other girls didn't, but I stuck to my course of action. At least the teacher would approve of me and I wouldn't get in trouble and be sent away somewhere awful, alone. The fear of transgressing that led me to always say "everything, please" drove my actions for the next thirty years. I reminded myself repeatedly to just say "yes" and "thank you" and "please" and, of course, the most valuable, "I would like to help, may I?" until they became ingrained responses. I could not risk drawing attention to myself in any way that was not positive, for fear that everyone would lean in closer and see my inner ugliness.

When I asked my mom why I didn't take a daily Flint-stones vitamin "like everybody else," she told me plainly that she cooked me nutritious meals every day and I didn't need extra vitamins. I hated that some of the girls' mothers told the teacher that their daughters had to be served skim milk and my mom didn't for me. I didn't know what skim milk was, but I thought if your mom insisted you have it at lunch, you were better cared for. I wondered why my mom never told the teacher that I could have a Dannon yogurt with "fruit on the bottom" for dessert. That was another special request a parent could make, and after our plates were cleared, some girls were presented with a cup of what-ever flavor was being served that day: blueberry, raspberry, strawberry, even coffee! I would stare at these seemingly more special girls as they mixed the fruit for a minute with their spoons and then stopped for a moment to dismantle the yogurt top, carefully peeling back the outer edges in order to free the round, coasterlike bit that would be saved and traded with the girls in the other grades. Some girls would carry their yogurt-top collection to the lunchroom in a small plastic sandwich bag. I didn't understand, but I wanted desperately for my mom to insist that I eat straw-berry yogurt so I could trade the tops. My mother served only plain yogurt, and it was not Dannon but Colombo, which I was sure was a brand from a foreign country where weirdos like my parents lived. In my family, we always put the plain Colombo yogurt on top of rice and whatever else we were eating for dinner. When I was sick, Mommy would spoon some of it out of the big container into a small bowl of rice for me. She'd add a little bit of salt and serve it to me with a spoon. I loved yogurt with rice and salt; it was my favorite food. But at school, I never wanted anyone to know that I ate it that way. It was one of my biggest secrets. At night, Mommy would put a whole huge container of Colombo yogurt into a special cloth bag and hang the bag over the sink. By the morning, all the water would be gone, and we would be left with a cloth bag full of *labne*, which she would then put in a dish and we would spoon some out for ourselves for breakfast, adding *za'atar* and olive oil, and scooping it up with warm Arabic bread. I loved it so much. It was another thing that no one at school could ever know about.

DESPITE THE ARABIC all around me, and the deep bond my parents had with their culture, I was never able to make the connection between the "fanatical Muslims" on TV, the rich oil princes who showed up in movies, or the magic carpets and belly dancers in books and pictures and anyone I knew or had ever known in my life. While my father was writing books about this very subject, I was looking at the images of Arabs on TV and in the movies and then looking back in the mirror, confounded. I had never seen anyone who looked like an Ali Baba cartoon, nor did I ever hear my parents use funny words to magically open doors. I did not know what a Muslim was, though I did know what a Jew and a Christian were. Like many American kids, I thought that Muslims were people from a faraway, exotic place. I once reenacted a scene from a cartoon for my mom. My friends and I had all seen the same one, and had spent the day making fun of it at school. When I got home, I wanted to make my mom laugh as we all had done. I got on my knees as the little brown men in the cartoon had done and undulated my torso up and down, raising and lowering my arms from the sky to the floor, over and over again, while saying the phrase that the cartoon characters had said: *"Ohhhhhh, salamiiiiiii. . . . Ohhhhhh, salamiiiiiiiiiiiiiiiiiiiiiiiii."* When I looked up, I realized my mother was not amused. She wasn't even impressed with the fact that I had gotten the pun in the use of the word "salami"! That sort of display of linguistic acumen had never failed to impress my parents! I knew I was in trouble, but I didn't know why. My mother's face tightened to a stern expression as she looked at me and said, "Naji, who taught you this? It is not funny. At all." She shook her head and tsked her way out of my room, without explaining why she was upset. I was ashamed at my behavior, but no less confused. I didn't know anyone who prayed like that, or looked like that. I thought it was funny.

I also knew that nobody in my family thought about or mentioned any kind of oil except the kind that was always on the dinner table. I had never seen a desert except on one vacation when we went to Tunisia, and I had never seen a camel anywhere but in the zoo. My parents did not pretend *not* to be Arabs, they just weren't at all like the ones I saw anywhere. There was absolutely no resemblance between the people I saw represented in the media and any single member of my extended family. Every so often, I would hear Baghdad or Beirut or Cairo mentioned in a movie or on a television program, and I would lean in curiously, hoping to see something that reminded me of my home, but I never once did.

Accordingly, even if I tried to identify with my culture and take pride in it, I couldn't find a place in it. Once, I was watching *I Dream of Jeannie*, and I perked up when I heard Jeannie say that she was from Baghdad. I knew that Baghdad was near Beirut and thus I was thrilled to discover that this gorgeous character was from the same part of the world as I was. But then for a moment, I considered: Jeannie was blond. She lived in a bottle and had her own TV show. She was also sexy, and showed her midriff, and had magic powers. Quite the opposite, I was dark, had absolutely no magic powers (believe me, I tried), and was far from sexy. I had also *tried* numerous times to rub the "magic" lantern that sat on our piano, but no genie ever came out of it to grant the three wishes that I made every single time (just in case the genie was invisible and mute). It seemed like no matter where I tried to fit in, I didn't.

My childhood was filled with moments like these. I was momentarily proud and excited to discover that someone famous was Arab, and then summarily heartbroken to realize that the existence of said person *as an Arab* did absolutely nothing to advance my place on earth. At the end of the day, that person was always somehow more American than I was, usually to the point that no one knew or cared about their "Arab-ness" (Danny Thomas, Casey Kasem, the guy who played Mel on *Alice*, the guy who dressed like a girl on *M*A*S*H*, Tiffany, Kristy McNichol, Paul Anka—who was *he* anyway?), or much more exotic and "ethnic" than I was (Cleopatra, Aladdin, Scheherazade, the guy holding up the airplane in whatever movie was on, the random Pakistani or Indian actor playing an "Arab" but clearly speaking Urdu or Farsi or nonsense in that same movie, Arafat, Gaddafi, and so on). There were also the "veiled women" I kept seeing in pictures or hearing about, but I never actually saw any in Lebanon, or within my family. There were the images of the entire post-Revolutionary population of Iran, and that Ayatollah dude who was *always* on television in the late '70s and early '80s.

Here is how I learned about Iranians, in the tenth grade:

"Mommy? What's the difference between an Iranian and a Persian?"

"Nothing."

"Well, how come some people always say 'Persian' and never say 'Iranian'?"

"Usually, that means that they are either not Muslim, or they left with the Shah and don't want to be associated with the current Islamic government, because America isn't friendly to Iran. It's like in Lebanon, the way the Maronite Christians sometimes call themselves Phoenicians instead of Arabs to distance themselves from the Muslims."

"Oh."

I considered all this for a moment, and then:

"Wait a minute. How come Iranians don't speak Arabic?"

"Because they are not Arabs."

"What? What are they, then?"

"Technically, they are Indo-Europeans, meaning they are ethnically closer to Indians and Europeans than they are to Arabs."

"And Arabs are . . . ?"

"Semites. Iranians are Aryans. But it's all bullshit anyway, Najla."

"Wait—Aryans? Like Hitler and skinheads?"

"Well, yes, not in that sense, but technically they are the same race. Hitler didn't mind Iranians, let's put it that way."

"So, like, if we had lived in Europe we would have been sent to a concentration camp with the Jews because we are Semites, but the Iranians would have been safe?"

"That's one way of looking at it, yes."

"Oh my God, that's so unfair," and in my classic fifteen-year-old whine and worldview, *"so typical of my luck!"*

THERE WAS ALSO the case of my "sisters"—two older girls at Chapin who had "the same last name" as I did. They were, in fact, sisters to each other, but no one seemed to understand that they had absolutely no connection to me. As the school was a small one, the younger girls knew the names of most of the older girls. Middle and upper school "ladies" often made announcements during Morning Prayers, or assembly. At some point very early on, I came to realize that it was taken as a given by most of my teachers and many of my friends that Sarah Sayeed and her older sister were *my* sisters as well. I quickly became exasperated at the immense effort I had to exert to dispel this rumor, and at the ridiculousness of it all. These girls were clearly South Asian, and while they did indeed look *like each*

other, neither one of them looked at all like me. We all had black hair and big brown eyes, yes, but the Sayeeds' features and mine were completely unalike. Our skin tones didn't even match. There were also the very plain facts: the Sayeeds and I had different parents, lived in different places, never spoke to each other, and last but definitely not least, spelled our surnames differently.

The assumption that the Sayeed sisters and I were related simply because we all seemed to be from somewhere east of the United States, some far-flung corner of the world whence few of our schoolmates came, reveals a startling lack of understanding among some highly educated Americans. I try to imagine that I might make a similar mistake today if I were to meet, say, a Danish person and a Dutch person. But when I try to pursue this idea in my head, I realize that even if I did think that Denmark and Holland were somehow "the same," I would probably still ask questions about each individual's life and his customs and his language. Ultimately, I would probably figure out that their homelands have very little to do with each other. Wasn't that sort of curiosity meant to be a large part of the very good education I was getting at my school? And yet, perhaps even more sadly, while I can wonder why no one at school asked me these sorts of questions, the startling truth is that I honestly didn't know the answers myself. Sure, I was able to maintain that *"I am not Indian!!!"* when a friend in kindergarten asked why I didn't have a dot on my forehead, but I couldn't assert much more.

Wadie may have been almost as confused as I was, but instead of avoiding the whole subject altogether, he would try to make sense of the bits and pieces of political opinion and thought he heard around him. The school he went to, Trinity, was an all-boys school on the Upper West Side. Despite its name, origins (it was established in the 1700s as a school for the choir boys of Trinity Church), and the huge cross that hung on the wall in its chapel, it was, by virtue of its location and its outstanding reputation, a lot more diverse than Chapin. Many of Wadie's classmates were Jewish, and most of them lived on the Upper West Side. Certainly, there were many families from the Upper East Side as well, but they were mostly exceptions to the rule. Wadie felt out of place at his school too, but for a reason I didn't yet understand: because he was an Arab boy surrounded by Jewish ones whose parents were wary of our family. The result was that, as I grew increasingly embarrassed by our background, Wadie grew more defiantly proud of it.

Once, when I was about five and Wadie seven, we were sitting in the back of our blue Buick as my father drove through Central Park at Christmastime. I remember looking at the lights that had been strung in the trees, feeling warm and safe in the car with my pretty coat and tights and my favorite shoes with bows on them. My father, as always, had tuned the radio to one of the classical music stations, WNCN or WQXR, which was broadcasting holiday music. I pressed my head against the window as I stared up toward the stars, and I began to sing along to a Christmas carol I had learned in school.

"Noel, Noel, Noel, Noel, born is the kiiiiing of *Iiiiis—*"

My pleasure was abruptly cut short by a swift smack on the arm.

"*Owww—Wad-ee—uh—*why'd you *hit* meeeeeee?*"

"*Naj*, you're *supposed* to say '*Occupied Palestine*'!!!"

I had no idea what he was talking about.

This was a song about Christmas, and we celebrated Christmas. So how come the other kids could say "Israel" and I had to say "Occupied Palestine"? I rubbed my wounded arm and appealed to my father for help. He dutifully chided Wadie for hitting me, and confirmed that I was allowed to sing the song as it was written. Mostly, I think my dad was amused by Wadie's attempt to impress him. My brother was only seven years old, but he had obviously picked up on the fact that my father, when discussing the question of Palestine with friends and colleagues, always referred to what we now call the West Bank and Gaza as "Occupied Palestine." This was well before any road maps or peace plans or lessons on political correctness. Feelings were still raw, the occupation was still relatively new, and monikers had not yet been set.

I have no doubt that the conversation in the car continued after this brief sibling spat. I have no doubt that my father carefully explained things to my brother, and that my brother listened intently, asked thousands of questions, and then went home and read books on the subject. I have no doubt that I was supposed to be listening to this argument so I would not make the same mistake and assume that references to ancient Israel in hymns, prayers, and scriptures were evidence of a Zionist prejudice, but I was gone. I was lost in the reverie of my Christmas daydream, imagining what baby Jesus looked like in his manger and wondering what were frankincense and myrrh.

When Wadie played the Egyptian baker who was sentenced to death in his fourth-grade production of *Joseph and the Amazing Technicolor Dreamcoat*, my mother offhandedly said something about his being typecast ("Oh, you see? The Arab child has to die so that the play can go on and so that the children of Israel can prevail . . . "). And though she may have been joking or, admittedly, may have been slightly paranoid (forgetting that at an all-boys school there are only so many plays you can do, and only as many potential lead actors as there are boys who can carry a tune), nevertheless, my brother heard, and went on to weigh the irony of my mother's musing. He got books and comics and educational LPs of the Bible, he sought out adults and grilled them on the ancient tribes and their descendant groups in the modern Middle East. Ultimately, Wadie learned the complete Biblical narrative of the history of the twelve tribes of Israel.

As for me, I preferred the story as Andrew Lloyd Webber imagined it. When I was nine, after we'd seen the show on Broadway and I'd gotten my parents to buy me the original cast recording, I'd sit by the record player and imagine myself Joseph, the pariah, hated by his eleven brothers, sold off as a slave only to overcome his miserable fate at the hands of the "hairy Ishmaelites" who had acquired him, to become a great and powerful Egyptian prince. Often, when my father was not home, I would play my favorite song at the end of side one repeatedly on his big hi-fi set in the living room. (I never had the courage to use anything of my dad's when he was there, and probably wasn't allowed to, now that I think about it.) I would sing along passionately and try to perform the way I had seen the actors on the Broadway stage do. Closing out the first act, Joseph, sentenced to life in an Egyptian jail cell, lamented his miserable fate. Even though he was to be locked away forever, imprisoned for all time, he knew he was somehow still special, because he was one of Israel's sons. The actor on the record merely accompanied me as I belted out my favorite part of the song, the part about the Children of Israel being promised a land of their own. At the top of my lungs I'd sing: "A la-and of our ooooooooooooown.'"

Whenever I reenacted this powerful scene, tears would well in my eyes, and chills would run through my body. I loved the dangerous feeling of stirring up my emotions. As soon as the last note of the song faded into silence and I heard the needle begin to skip on the paper center of the LP, I would promptly rise to move the needle back to the start of the song, and do it all again.

Wadie, usually in the next room watching football or something, would yell at me to "turn that off—it's propaganda!" I now think he said that mainly because I sang badly and the noise was annoying. But at the time, I felt shame at my sincere love of the musical and thought I must be doing something really inappropriate, at odds with where I came from and who I was supposed to be. If I were really trying to find myself in the play, it should have been as one of the Ishmaelites, the "hairy crew" that bought Joseph from his brothers, enslaved him, imprisoned him, and lived in plenty as the Israelites wasted away during seven years of famine.

I just wanted to be normal, and to me, being normal meant being able to sing anything you wanted. I was constantly confused, and I sulked and pouted for years about my family's insistence on being so serious, weird, and contrary about *everything*.

At the same time, however, I wanted desperately to understand what Wadie and my parents seemed to understand. I knew I *would* understand if someone took the time to explain things to me carefully. There was no doubt in my mind that I loved my home and my family. There was no food I wanted to eat but my mom's; there were no people I really wanted to be around other than my parents, my brother, and our extended family and friends. I loved everything about my home life, even though it was ostensibly different from my friends'. But I wanted to know more about where I was from, so I could defend it. I wanted to know what it meant that I was an Ishmaelite and not an Israelite, and I wanted to know why, in the musical at least, they were the bad guys. I wanted to know why I seemed to be the only Ishmaelite in New York, and I wanted to be able to explain to outsiders why not all of us were bad. I just didn't know how.

Our house was always filled with people; we had an enormous extended family that consisted not only of people who were actual blood relatives but also of family friends who popped in and out, always bringing with them stories of travels and adventures around the world. Every night of the week I looked forward to gathering at the dining room table with my brother, my parents, and whatever unexpected friend of theirs might drop by for dinner. Before we ate, however, we would watch the evening news on television. To me, the opening music of a Walter Cronkite or Dan

Rather or Peter Jennings broadcast was the signal that my parents were home and I was safe and part of a family. My parents would each have a glass of beer as they watched. Mommy would go in and out of the kitchen to check on dinner, and Daddy would eat peanuts out of the Planters jar. I'd join him, sticking my entire hand into the jar to retrieve a handful of their saltiness, and then I would take his beer glass off its coaster and take a little sip, making sure he saw me and smiled. It was our little secret, that. (I don't know if I liked beer, but the first time I had a sip, I acted as if I did. Wadie didn't like it, so I at least pretended to. I wanted Daddy's letting me have a little taste to be a special moment for us to share.)

Even if I thought the news was slightly boring and didn't completely understand what was being discussed, I paid attention every single night. I think that this is part of the reason that, despite my isolation at school, I was still able to conceive of a larger world, one beyond school and New York and the East or West Side. Though I didn't understand the intricacies of each story, I was concerned about the starving children in Cambodia, and the Iran-Iraq War, and the Falkland Islands, and the Sandinistas, and all the other things that came up in a little box to the right of Dan Rather's head every single evening. I asked a million questions. I can't say I ever fully grasped what I was being taught, but I liked to listen. My parents seemed to know about everything, and they could always explain every situation from a different perspective than the news reporter. I was fascinated by that ability; they always managed to understand something that I never would have thought of. I was curious as to how to do that. They also really seemed to care about other people, and they talked about what could be done to help them. I admired that so much; they took the time every night to talk about the problems of people thousands of miles away, people they would most likely never meet. My heart would swell with love for my parents when I listened to them talk about the stories on the news.

Our dinner guests would do the same. I certainly didn't know that I was often learning about the world from UN delegates, people who had fought for Algerian independence, journalists who had been kidnapped and subsequently escaped, and people who were changing the course of human thought in the twentieth century. I did know that I loved to listen to them talk. At home, and by example, I learned to listen, and to hear things from different sides. While at school I felt that I was being forced to fit into one idea of what was "right" and what was "wrong," at home I rejoiced in the feelings of comfort and solidarity that the awareness of being part of a larger, varied world brought. Even if I felt that I couldn't reconcile these two disparate worlds, I never actually let go of my firm footing in the one

I learned about and felt part of at home—the larger, more complicated, real one.

I also learned about the rest of the world by listening to my parents engage in conversation with anyone and everyone they encountered. My father was very friendly and loved to chat with strangers, be they doormen, waiters, salespeople, cabdrivers, movie stars, princes, CEOs, or doctors. He wanted to know everyone's story, everyone's history, everyone's political leanings, no matter where they came from or what they did for a living.

One year we took a vacation to Jamaica and stayed at a resort in Montego Bay. It was the kind of vacation many of my friends from school had also been on, but I can't say that any other twelve-year-old I knew ended up learning as much about Jamaican politics as I did while frolicking on the beach. We rented a bungalow that came with a cook, Mabel. Although she seemed cold at first, she softened when my mom encouraged her to prepare a rabbit dish for dinner, explaining that she and my father wanted her to prepare Jamaican specialties for us to try. My mother also said that she and my father grew up eating rabbit. Surprised to learn that my parents were from the Middle East, Mabel began to ask them questions about their lives. They responded eagerly, and a lively conversation ensued. At some point I remember my father asking Mabel if she supported

Michael Manley, the former prime minister of Jamaica who talked of "giving power to the people." When he told her of his own admiration for the Jamaican leader, Mabel smiled broadly. I watched the scene unfold with curiosity, and I felt my heart fill with warmth as I observed my father and mother's effortless engagement with this young Jamaican woman. And I came to understand that the world could be a smaller and less hostile place if you engaged with others the way my parents did.

Ironically, despite my desperation to fit in at school, I loved the way my parents seemed to blend in seamlessly anywhere in the world and could make connections between anything and everything. Of course, I couldn't always reconcile the cultural richness of my home and family life with the more black-and-white world of my immediate environment, but I knew I was lucky.

I was named after my great-aunt Najla. Once, when I was very small, Auntie Najla had given me green playing cards with my name printed on them, and I treasured them for the normalcy they signified: if someone sold "Najla" cards, it must be a normal name.

To my daddy, I was "Naji Baji, pudding and pie," who "kissed the girls" (or was it the boys?) "and made them cry." Daddy had made up that nickname when I was little, and I always thought the nursery rhyme actually went that way. I didn't know about anyone named Georgie Porgie until I heard the real version during my teenage years. (I think I still assumed someone had gotten that song from my dad, and changed it to fit kids named George.) Jiddo

Emile hated that Daddy called me Naji (in Arabic, Naji is a male name, so calling me that was kind of like calling me "Mike") rather than Naj-jool-lie, but in my mind, the fact there was a *song* about my name (or was it actually about *me?*) reinforced my confidence in its intrinsic value and instilled a boundless pride. Naji became the nickname that stuck.

As I got older, I realized that my parents had had plenty of pronounceable options in naming their children. They *could* have given me an Arabic name that was close to an English one, I thought, as I considered the Mayas, Salmas, Mariannas, and Dinas in my own family. Even my mother and father had normal names! The names Mariam and Edward would have been a lot more useful for two kids in New York City than they had been for my mother and father in the Middle East, where they had grown up. My dad's sisters were Rosemarie, Jean, Joyce, and Grace, and his mother, Hilda. His father had been Wadie, but it had "turned into" William when he came to America. (I supposed that since I was *born* in America my name hadn't had the chance to turn into anything.) Two of my mom's three brothers had pretty easy names too: Ramzi and Sami were at least names you heard in America once in a while. I found out at some point that my parents had seriously considered calling me Emilia, after both my grandfather

Emile and my father's favorite aunt, Melia, and I was crushed when they told me.

"I could have been *Emmy*!!! I *hate you*!!!"

I spent hours of my time trying to come up with more adaptable names for myself. If I spelled my name backward, for instance, I could be Spanish (well, kind of)—"Aljan Dias"! Or, since one of my nicknames was Naj, I could just reverse that and be "Jan," like Jan Brady. Nothing was more American than *The Brady Bunch*, so I quietly called myself Jan in secret. Then when I was a little older I thought I should go by "Lala" and announced it a couple of times, but no one ever complied with my wish. Some people thought my name sounded like an inverted version of "Angela," and I really liked that option. I tried to say my name fast sometimes so people would hear "Angela" and not follow their "Hi, what's your name?" with the inevitable "*What* is it??? Oh . . . uh-huh, okay . . . that's *interesting* . . ." (*Fake smile*)

Wadie was on his own to figure out his American name. Poor dude: Wadie is not so easy to play around with.

My parents—especially my mother—tried to relieve my mortification by telling me that it was my unique name that made me special:

"Your name may not be Jennifer or Laura or Amy, but your name is *beautiful* because it has a *meaning*."

"It does? What does it mean?!!!"

"It means 'big black eyes like a cow'!"

Apparently, that is a compliment.

Unfortunately, my heightened and growing awareness of my physical awkwardness coincided perfectly with the growing violence and political instability in the Middle East. As the '80s continued on, the region in general and Lebanon in particular became synonymous with all that was uncivilized, evil, barbaric, violent, and foreign in the world. I tried desperately to fit in at school but at the same time to remain loyal to all that I treasured and loved about my home and my family. I gleaned from both pop culture and my friends' offhanded comments that I ought to *avoid* being connected to Beirut as it appeared on television and in the movies, I ought to be quiet about the fact that my parents preferred President Carter to President Reagan, and that they took me to protests on weekends instead of to "the country."

But my family's overwhelmingly lefty politics frequently crept into my life as an otherwise "normal" private-school girl in New York City. I found myself struggling to please my parents by trying to understand the world the way they did, and by performing well in school. At the same time, I was desperate to be accepted by both my classmates and my teachers. I was young, and confused, and torn between complex worlds I didn't understand, and as a result I became more shy, more quiet, and more comfortable escaping into the fantasy world of my books and the complex imaginary realms I would create in the privacy of my room.

In January of 1981, fifty-two American hostages who had been held captive in Iran for more than a year were released. At school, a television set was wheeled into our classrooms so we could watch the historical moment together. We were only in the first grade, so I don't think any of us understood what was actually happening, but it was made very clear to us by our teachers that we should be very, very happy. I knew I wasn't from Iran, and I knew that anyone who held hostages had to be a bad guy, so I was thrilled by the dramatic release of the American hostages and felt goose bumps all over my body as we watched. I bounced home from school. I couldn't wait to tell Mommy how happy I was. I breathlessly recounted for her what I had gotten to watch on TV (at school!). She smiled, listened, and then decided to further my education:

"Naji, do you know that the reason the American hostages were released today was because Algeria, an *Arab* country, stepped in and helped the Americans talk to the Iranians?"

"No. But they are Americans and we are Americans, so I am happy, Mommy."

"They are people, like everyone in the world, and you

should be happy, but I also want you to be aware that there were Arabs who helped make it happen, because you are an Arab."

"*Mommy!!!* You spoil *everything!*"

I ran to my room and slammed the door. As a six-year-old, I could only understand being happy or sad, American or Iranian. Why did the Arabs have to get involved and mix everything up?

In the summer of 1981, my mother decided she wanted to go somewhere new for vacation. We skipped Lebanon that year and went to Tunisia instead. We spent three weeks on the beach and at the pool. I'd jump on my dad's back when we swam in the sea and declare that I was taking a ride on "Edward Airlines." We stayed in an enormous house that had a pool and a grand piano that Daddy loved to play before dinner. We walked through the city with Daddy's friend Mahmoud Darwish, who was a famous poet. He enchanted me with his words and charm; he gave Wadie a beautiful piece of quartz that still sits in his bedroom at home. We went to an outdoor seafood restaurant, and cats prowled around our table looking for scraps. Mahmoud began to tell me a story. I felt like a princess when he talked to me. As I listened, mesmerized, I forgot about the forkful of fish in my right hand until one of the cats jumped over my shoulder and devoured it. I screamed. Everyone laughed. I loved Tunis.

We didn't go to Beirut in the summer of 1982 either. It was too dangerous, because the Israelis had invaded. Wadie, ten and a half years old, went to sleepaway camp. Daddy had a teaching commitment at Northwestern University, and so I went with my parents to Evanston, Illinois. I did cartwheels in the living room, trying to get Mommy and Daddy's attention. But all they did was watch the news and eat nuts and look worried. I hated that summer. I was so lost. My parents had chosen a day camp for me where each camper would choose to spend the summer doing only gymnastics, soccer, or swimming. They knew I loved gymnastics and thought I would love the camp. I did, in theory, but I didn't know a soul. I watched a TV movie about Nadia Comaneci four times in one week and tried to become her by wearing my hair in pigtails and practicing my floor routines again and again. Mommy and Daddy still watched the news and worried.

We went back to New York. I went to another day camp. One morning in the pool, I attempted to engage an Israeli girl on the topic of our warring nations, without letting on that I was Arab:

Me: So, Yael, have you heard of any interesting wars going on lately?

(I recognize that my lead-in question was hardly transparent, but I was seven! Besides, Yael suspected nothing, so I apologize for nothing.)

Yael: Yes, well, Israel is fighting in Lebanon to save everyone from the Palestinians.

Me: Oh, really? *(Surprised face)* What do you mean?

Yael continued to give me a lesson on the situation as she saw it, and I listened, never once letting on that I was Lebanese Palestinian. In retrospect, though, I remember it vividly, along with the racing heartbeat in my chest. I am not sure why I began this conversation. I recall wanting to talk about the war, thinking I might as well confront the elephant in the room, while simultaneously wanting to stay outside of the conversation, pretending it had no bearing on my life. It seemed dangerous but necessary that I find a way to talk about what was going on, even though I didn't understand anything about the conflict. I knew Yael would have an opinion because I knew she was from Israel. I knew her opinion would be different from mine, but at least it would be an opinion. The subject seemed so important at home. I thought I *must* try to find a way to talk about it the way my parents did.

Six months later, the children's ward of St. Luke's Hospital became Wadie's home for four long weeks. One Saturday during ice hockey practice, the blade of another kid's skate had somehow pressed into my brother's foot, causing him to develop a severe bone infection, osteomyelitis. Throughout Wadie's hospital stay, Mommy would show up at his bedside every morning at seven a.m. to give him breakfast from home. Then she'd go to work from nine a.m. to five p.m. Then she'd return to the hospital for the evening. She'd make him dinner too. At three thirty, Frank the bus driver would drop me off in front of the hospital with Patricia, who was always dropped there after school to be with her mom, a nurse. I would hang out in the hospital as Wadie received visitors and presents and candy and potato chips. I would show our family friends my old room, the one where, two months earlier, I'd spent a grand total of twenty minutes before I underwent a minor surgical procedure on my foot. I wanted everyone to know I had been in the hospital first.

I wandered the hallways; the hospital smell made me want to throw up. I befriended the other patients, but I hated the hospital. It scared me. So many of the kids I met there were sick or abused in ways that underscored the dangers of the world. A lot of them were poor too; St. Luke's served a mixed range of neighborhoods, including Harlem. My green-and-white-striped uniform made me self-conscious in a new way, embarrassed by my privilege, whereas I'd felt low-class just an hour earlier at school.

❧

WADIE FINALLY CAME HOME, and then spent another two and a half weeks in bed there. I would run home after school, worried, wanting to make sure he was feeling okay. We'd sit in Mommy and Daddy's room all afternoon, watching MTV. (Since Wadie was still sick, we got away with normally forbidden things like that.) Leaning on his good leg in the blue pajamas he always wore, Wadie would cradle one of his crutches in his arms, and with surprising authenticity, he'd strum along with The Police, The Kinks,

David Bowie, or Madness. I was happy that Wadie was at home with us again. The four of us needed to be together to stay safe.

That summer, though, my eyes were further opened to the complexities of our lives and the conflicts of the world. I would never again feel as safe and protected as I had upon Wadie's return to our family nest.

Despite the continued unrest in Lebanon, we had taken a chance that year and had gone to visit Jiddo Emile and Teta Hilda in Beirut. We left my father in Paris, whence he would go on to Geneva to attend a UN conference. When I asked my mother why he wasn't coming to Beirut, she replied honestly: "It's not safe for him as a Palestinian." I wondered why we couldn't put a costume on him and hide him in the trunk of the car.

The second our plane touched down in Beirut, passengers erupted into their customary applause heralding our safe arrival. Behind us, a woman thanked God for allowing us to land safely and in peace. My mother murmured, "It's safer on the plane than it is outside," and then looked sorry when she realized I'd heard her. Wadie and I sensed the imminent danger, but I don't think anyone, including my mother, realized just how close it was. Before we even exited the aircraft, we were jolted forward by a loud *boom*. A man laughed cynically. My mother grabbed my hand with such a squeeze I can still feel its sting. Clutching Wadie and me to her side, repeating phrases like *"Ya Allah"* and *"Ya Rab,"* she led us off the plane and onto the terminal bus with such care one would have thought we were infants. The sun was setting and the bombs beginning. We heard more loud noises, but we could now see smoke coming from the mountains, soldiers with rifles crouched on the tarmac, and chaos brewing inside the terminal. I kept looking from my mother to Wadie to the smoke-filled mountains, trying to figure out how to react. We would be safe, wouldn't we? I remember thinking, We were *Americans* after all. We would be okay, always. That's what my parents had promised.

After getting our bags and heading toward the meeting area, we caught site of the top of Jiddo Emile's head. He was very tall and very bald, so we could always find him in a crowd. Just above his head was the head of a little boy, who was sitting on his shoulders. Wadie and I smiled with excitement: that must be our new baby cousin, Shadi! For a moment, gripped with the thrill of being back among family members, we forgot the noises we heard outside and the commotion swirling around us within the airport. My mother, however, on seeing Shadi bouncing up and down on Jiddo's shoulders as he waved us over calmly and happily, began to freak out. Up until that moment, I had never ever seen my mother lose her cool. Now she started yelling at her father, our jiddo, and then at my uncle Sami, who was just coming in from the parking garage. She was hysterical. (I learned that word—"hysterical" in English and *"emhestera"* in Arabic—that very day.) She didn't understand how they could be so calm, how they could bring a one-year-old baby out in this bombing. Jiddo and Khalo Sami told her to calm down, and they smiled and laughed and hugged us. Wadie and I followed their example, and laughed and smiled with them and told Mommy to calm down. We drove home to Jiddo's, where the rest of our family waited to greet us as they always did. After a couple of hours of stuffing our faces with food and our small bodies with love, Jiddo and the others sent us off to bed. Although everything seemed the same in some ways, I knew by looking at Wadie's face as he led me into the bedroom we shared that our vacation was going to end before it even began.

I cannot tell you who was fighting whom or what faction was clashing with what other faction that week. I could look it up, but in the end it doesn't really matter. I can tell you that there were bombs and gunshots downstairs, outside our building, around the corner. I can describe for you how we spent a week in the stairwell in the center of our building—the safest place—as the shells continued to fall. I can tell you about the lack of electricity in the entire building and therefore in the stairwell, and about the dark that was beyond any darkness I had ever known before. The experience was enough for me to understand that every war ever fought, every violent act ever committed, and every trauma any child has ever endured is utterly horrifying, and that's all you need to know for now.

In Switzerland, Daddy knew we were in danger before we even landed in Lebanon. Within moments of his arrival at the conference, he ran into a Lebanese friend who asked about his wife and children. This man had ties to someone involved in the current battle, the one that we'd been caught in, and he told my dad that we were going to have to make plans to get out of Lebanon just as soon as we landed. A second flight to Beirut, from Jordan, had been grounded in Amman. The Air France flight we had been on was the last one allowed into the country before the airport had been forced to close.

Mommy tried to get us out on the first plane possible, but there were no plans to reopen the airport anytime soon. A day or so later, Jiddo Emile heard from a friend that Middle East Airlines had promised every passenger who had booked a flight to Mecca for the hajj that they would get them there, no matter what the circumstances. The airline followed through on their promise by chartering a boat to get all the would-be pilgrims from Lebanon to Cyprus safely. Once in Cyprus, they would be able to board flights to Saudi Arabia and complete their pilgrimage. Jiddo Emile somehow found us places on this boat.

The next day, Mommy and Wadie went to the building

next door to ours to send Daddy a telex saying we were going to leave. (Mommy went to send a telex; Wadie went to borrow a Tintin comic from my cousin Kamal.) They were almost killed by a shell. It landed in front of the building they were in seconds before they came out the door. No one told me, but I could tell from the way they acted when they returned that something bad had happened. It filled me with even more terror, something I had not even considered possible.

The night before we left, I went into Mommy's bed. Her balcony door was open because there was no air-conditioning, no electricity. As the curtains fluttered behind me, I shivered and shook in my nonexistent sleep. I felt the breeze graze my back and knew for certain the bombs would get me as I lay there, vulnerable. But I was frozen in terror, shivering and shaking, teeth chattering. I wanted desperately to move to the other side, to switch places with Mommy, have her wrap her arms around me and keep me safe—but then she would feel the bombs, on her back, I reasoned, and *she* would die! "I can't lose Mommy. I can't lose Mommy," I repeated to myself. "I'd rather die than lose Mommy. I'm so, so, so scared."

We got to the port at four in the afternoon. I didn't want to leave Jiddo Emile. I announced to my mother that I was staying with him. He was so happy that I loved him, that I loved Beirut enough to want to stay there no matter what the circumstances. I sometimes wonder if I had some feeling or premonition that I would never see him again. I finally heeded my mother's call to decide quickly whether I was really staying. I think she knew there was no way I would leave her side. I got out of the car. Wadie, Mommy, and I took our place in line at the dock, waiting alongside the other very frightened, confused passengers. I stared at the big cruise ship waiting in the harbor. It had a woman's face on it, the exact same emblem that adorned the "Love Boat" from TV. I pulled on Wadie's arm: "We are going on the *Pacific Princess!*" The juxtaposition of life-threatening explosions and a luxurious TV-show cruise ship was preposterous. Yet, having just witnessed such unimaginable violence, the idea that the world of a TV show might physically materialize in front of us no longer seemed impossible. Continued patience seemed worth it now; I was relieved. It grew dark. At some time well past midnight, we boarded a boat, but it was not the "Love Boat." It was a small, overbooked ferry that had pulled into the port alongside it. We did not have rooms to stay in since we were last-minute emergency additions to the passenger list, but a kind man had offered us his cabin so that my brother and I might try to sleep. I couldn't sleep; the room was metal and smelled of metal; even the mattress seemed to be made of metal. I couldn't breathe either; the air in the lower compartment was thick and salty and heavy. Mommy took me up to the

deck for air. I was seasick. I vomited again and again, over
the side of the boat. We stayed there the whole night. Soon,
all of the pilgrims, dressed in white robes, came up to the
deck to pray. I had no idea what they were or what they
were doing. I didn't understand. I didn't know Muslim or
Christian or Jew. I didn't know anything. The whole week
had been so surreal. They looked like fluttering angels, and
they remain in my memory that way.

I suppose it was after that summer, when I returned to New York and started middle school at Chapin, that I began to realize that even if I didn't entirely identify with Arabs as they were presented to me in America, I actually was one of them just as much as I was an American from New York. And while I don't think I made any clear connections about this in my head, I know that I was suddenly more acutely aware of the fact that no one in my school had spent her summer in a place and a situation that was even remotely like where I'd spent mine. After my escape from Beirut under bombs, my difference at school started to feel deeper, sadder, darker, and more incomprehensible to my nine-year-old mind than ever before.

At the very beginning of fourth grade we read a book called *The Endless Steppe* at school. It was the true story of a Polish girl named Esther who was sent to work on a potato farm in Siberia with her family during World War II. Esther's family was Jewish and they were wealthy. According to the story, the Russians took them away from their home to live in poverty and servitude in a bleak, faraway land because they were "capitalists." Though the story was not about a European Jewish family that was sent to a Nazi concentration camp, like the diary of Anne Frank, it did make clear that part of the excuse for the family's banishment was their belief in Judaism.

We read *The Endless Steppe* at Chapin in part because the author had survived, grown up, married, moved to New York City, and sent her own daughter to our school. So every year, Esther Hautzig would come to Chapin to meet the fourth-grade class after they'd finished reading her book. I remember loving it very much, and taking comfort in Esther's portrayal of the family's deep love and support for one another, which seemed a significant part of how and why they were able to survive their years in Siberia. At the time, I did not find any parallels between young Esther's life and my own. Looking back on the book now, I am somewhat amazed by the similarities between her descriptions of a happy childhood surrounded by family and all the very best things money can buy, and my own memories as I have recounted them in these pages. And though I read this book just a few months after the horrific experience of leaving my beloved Lebanon as it was being bombed, interestingly, I never made any of these now strikingly obvious connections when I was nine.

What I do remember distinctly is meeting Esther Hautzig one sunny afternoon in an assembly hall at school. Although her book was not about her survival in a Nazi concentration camp, it led us into class discussions and assignments about World War II and the Holocaust.

We'd spent so much of our early years asking, "Are you Jewish or Christian?" that I knew already which handful of girls in my class were Jewish. Now some of them talked about their grandparents having been in concentration camps, or having fled Europe. That history moved me deeply. But in my classmates themselves, I always had trouble discerning any real differences between the Jewish girls and the Christian ones. All I really knew about Jewish people was that they didn't believe that Jesus was the son of God, and that they got presents on eight consecutive nights for Hanukkah. Some of my Jewish friends had Christmas trees in their houses too, right next to the menorah, which I found confusing and possibly unfair.

But it was in the fourth grade that I also became best friends with Caroline, who was Jewish. I spent lots of time at her house after school, and I always felt loved and happy.

Caroline's parents treated me like their own daughter, in many ways. But whenever Caroline talked about her half sister, who was sixteen and lived in Israel with her mom, I wanted to run and hide. Caroline always made her sound so cool, but I was quite relieved to never meet her myself. I was convinced that she would hate me because I was Lebanese and Palestinian, and would tell Caroline to do the same. I didn't want her sister, whom she idolized, to tell Caroline the truth about me, even if I wasn't exactly sure what that was.

I suppose that my summer experience in Lebanon, along with the fact that I was getting older and starting to make some connections about the larger world, jarred me into understanding that Israel, which was in a war with Lebanon, was a place for Jewish people. And Jewish people had suffered terribly in World War II, which had occurred recently enough to have affected some of my Jewish classmates' grandparents. Obviously, I was still too young to understand the nuances of the situation beyond the "good guys" and "bad guys," but I felt sympathy for the Jewish people for what they had endured. And while my feelings of sympathy were not connected in any way to my being Arab, they nevertheless made me feel horribly guilty about exactly that.

When I went to visit a summer-camp friend in Connecticut, and I heard her mom tell her grandmother that my mom was from *"Leb-a-non"* slowly, deliberately, a little loudly, and followed by an exaggerated smile, I wanted to disappear. *Maybe her grandmother is deaf? Or foreign,* I thought quickly, trying to give her mom the benefit of the doubt, but I somehow knew that the change in pitch in her voice had more to do with a wariness about my being from the country that was at war with "the Jews." I wished I were dead. I wished people didn't have to know, that they could just hear my mom's accent and acknowledge it, but not ask where she was from. As much as they liked her, and me, and all of us, I could tell that many people were disgusted by what they thought about the people from her home country, and I felt ashamed.

Of course, I felt especially scared that people would find out that I was from Lebanon when I was in a Jewish home. I would apologize for everything I did and said and try to keep quiet all the time. I was so very sorry. For what, I had no idea, but the feeling was real. Whenever I walked by the synagogue on 87th and Madison on my way to after-school acting classes, I'd keep my head down and pray that no one would see me. I was sorry for that too, but I was never sure why.

It got to the point that whenever anyone would ask where my parents were from, what kind of name I had, or what my brother's name was, I would reply with one stock answer: "I don't know." My friends never pressed me further when I responded this way, but their parents would often look at me a little strangely, as if they knew I was hiding something, and then, even if they came over to hug me, I would act as shy and elusive as possible, so they would never ask anything more. One day, one of my friend's mothers said to my own, "Where are you from? I asked Najla, but she said she didn't know, that she 'forgot.'" I felt my mother's eyes burn into my own. She didn't seem to be mad; she looked surprised, stunned even. Of course, she knew that I knew she was from Lebanon as well as I knew my own name. I lowered my gaze and I muttered, "Yeah, yeah, I forgot," as Mommy gracefully answered the question: "I am from Lebanon."

"Ohhhhhhhhhhhhhhhhhh, yeah," I said happily, feigning a look that made it seem as if I'd suddenly remembered the name of her country, "*that's* what it is!"

I confess I don't remember this particular instance (though I do remember many others just like it), but my mom always tells this story to illustrate when exactly *she* realized how difficult it had become for me to be an American with Arab parents. She recalls not understanding at all why I was pretending not to know the answer to a very simple question I had answered correctly and readily many times before. Later that week, it occurred to her that I must have been embarrassed.

"A few days later, I just suddenly realized, 'Oh my God,

for Naji it must be so painful to be growing up in this country at a time when Arabs are really being vilified.' I was, you
know, just sad for you. This whole business of 'crazy, violent
Arabs and Muslims' was relatively new still, and I had certainly not grown up ever hearing that stuff, so it didn't even
dawn on me until a few days later that that was why you
pretended you didn't know."

I kept to myself even more, and was as quiet as I could
be. I didn't want any unnecessary attention paid to me if it
meant that people were going to ask where my parents were
from. The thought of people's expectant faces dropping to
an awkward, uncomfortable, somewhat disappointed expression upon hearing the answer was too much to bear.

In the summer of 1984, between the fourth and fifth
grades, I spent my first of seven consecutive summers at a
sleepaway camp on Cape Cod. It had become clear to me
that I wasn't going to be spending my summers in Beirut
anymore, both because of the war and because I was old
enough to go to sleepaway camp with other children my
age. I suppose I knew intuitively that from now on I would
have to be as American as possible to fit in and stay happy,
and camp was the perfect environment in which to do
so, especially since I was on my own to create an identity
for myself. My camp was, much like my school, for relatively privileged children and teenagers, and because of
its location, and its emphasis on sailing and other water

sports, it attracted many of the same types of families as my school did.

One evening during that first summer, my parents told me over the phone that I had won a citywide contest that I did not even know I had entered. I actually did not register exactly what it was they told me because I was so supremely focused on being homesick and relishing the love in their voices that I barely heard what they said, but I remember thinking that they might be confused, and mixing me up with my brother. On parents' weekend, the subject came up again. This time around, I heard what they said. But instead of getting up excitedly and asking for my prize, as most ten-year-olds might do, I replied straightforwardly, working very carefully to keep any hint of a whine out of my voice: "I told you. I did not *enter* a contest, so I couldn't have won one." My calm demeanor hid a deep anxiety and panic; without even asking for more information or proof or momentarily entertaining the notion that I might have forgotten about said contest, I anxiously set about fixing things. It was imperative that I clear things up and that I make sure my parents alert the people in charge at once! Whatever award-worthy achievement had been mistaken for something I had done was most definitely *not* mine! I was certain I had not won anything, because my embarrass-ment over being Arab had begun to spill over into my self-confidence in every other area of my life; I was definitely not the best artist in my class! Had I known its meaning, "mediocre" would have been the word I'd have used to describe my talents in just about everything I did or said at that time in my life. There was no way I had done a better drawing than the at least twenty other girls I could think of who were better artists than I. The thought of winning something I didn't really deserve also terrified me because if I became the center of attention for something that wasn't even that good, then the rest of my classmates would hate me. And then, when they were mean to me, they would tease me and shun me for being Arab, and say, "Of course she cheated to win, she's an *Arab*."

My mind began to spin into despair along these lines as my parents explained more, and then I remembered an art class from earlier in the year in which the in-class assignment was to draw a picture that could be used as a traffic safety poster you might see on a bus or subway. I'd had no idea what to do. I knew whatever idea I came up with would be stupid or wrong or "Arab" or weird. When the teacher, Ms. Burrows, came over to me and asked if I needed some help, I managed to say:

"Well, um, well it's dumb, but maybe I think I want to draw a girl tying her shoe in the middle of the street and then there's, like, a car? Coming toward her? But she doesn't notice. So, like, she's about to get hit. But the car isn't there yet. Or something . . ."

I drew my picture exactly as I had described it, though still feeling uncertain. Toward the end of class, I looked up and noticed that absolutely every other student had drawn decapitated heads rolling down the street and dismembered limbs scattered about, or girls with Band-Aids on their faces and blood gushing from their battered, beaten, flattened bodies. I was mortified. I had completely misunderstood the assignment because I was a stupid Arab from the West Side, and Ms. Burrows hadn't stopped me!

Now my parents were telling me that my drawing was the best one, that it had been chosen from *hundreds* of other drawings by fourth-graders all over New York City. My mom proudly explained that it had been singled out "by a *psychiatrist*, who thought that it was a very sensitive, clever, and effective picture! *And* was really moved because it was *the only drawing* that did not depict one single image of blood or violence."

MOMMY GRINNED from ear to ear as she continued explaining to me that this psychiatrist had made sure the rest of the selection committee saw my brilliant oeuvre and that they all took into account its subtle, sophisticated brilliance. For a moment, I was pleased with myself, or maybe I was just pleased with my parents' smiling faces. They brought out a copy of the final poster and asked me to sign it for them so that they could frame it and hang it at home. I stared at it blankly, and was suddenly miserable and scared again.

Underneath what was unmistakably my drawing (even worse than I remembered—the girl was missing a nose, and her hand looked more like a foot) were the words *Be Alert!* staring back at me, menacingly. "Be Alert!"? That was absolutely *not* my idea! My caption had been something literal like "Don't tie your shoes in the middle of the street." Now I was really concerned. These posters had obviously been printed by the dozens and were about to end up all over the public buses and subways of New York City, and some little girl who was richer and blonder and prettier than I would end up *suing me* for stealing her slogan and sticking it under my drawing.

I was dying inside. "Be Alert!" sounded like something a grown-up would say! It was also far too concise to be something I would come up with. And under my noseless quadruped, in all caps and a bold black font, it seemed to be yelling at me.

"I didn't say that. That's not what I said," I repeated endlessly for the rest of the day, perhaps hoping that on the 378th refrain they'd hear what I was saying.

I was petrified of being the center of attention. I was still too ugly and hairy and Arab to be put on display. Everyone would have an invitation to mock me and my "Arab-ness," which I had not yet figured out how to hide. People (Jewish people!) would know where my parents were from and be mortified. But I couldn't tell my parents any of that.

The actual prize I was meant to receive for my stunning display of artistry and sensitivity was twofold: I would have the honor of seeing my poster all over the New York City streets, buses, subways, and billboards, *and* I would get to meet the mayor of New York City—Edward I. Koch. Alas, neither of these two great big things happened, unless the posters were put only on the subways, buses, and billboards in the four boroughs I never went to, which is possible, I suppose.

As for Mayor Koch, even though his home was just across the street from my school, he was "too busy" to ever schedule a meeting with me. My parents surmised in their usual partly humorous, partly serious way that "it's because you're *Arab*" (the mayor was an outspoken supporter of Israel), which only further supported my anxieties but, ironically, freed me from the exposure I had come to fear most.

A few months later, my homeroom teacher told me that during lunch I was to take my tray up to Room 3½ (I distinctly remember it being the only room on a half floor, which made it all the more surreal) and "talk to a woman." My friend Stephanie, feeling my unease, smiled reassuringly and said, "I bet it's because of your poster! You are *so lucky*!!!"

As it turned out, I was being sent to the school psychiatrist to deal with my "anxiety" (the word I had recently started hearing my parents whisper behind my back).

I went to Mrs. Rosenman's office on a weekly basis after that, with my lunch tray, and talked about nothing. This is how things usually went:

MRS. R: So, Najla, how was your weekend?

ME: Fine.

MRS. R: What did you do?

ME: Nothing.

MRS. R: Did you . . . go shopping?

ME: Okay, yes.

MRS. R: Did you buy anything nice?

ME: Yes.

MRS. R: Oh, tell me what you got!

ME: I don't remember.

That was about as detailed as things got. Funnily, the one time I thought of something to say, it was about how I had just learned from a girl in my class that last names that end in "man" are usually Jewish names, and so I knew that meant that she, Mrs. Rosenman, was Jewish. But I held back. For some reason I knew that I shouldn't say that to her, even if I just wanted to show off my wisdom.

From the school psychiatrist, I progressed to the real psychiatrist. A few months after my first visit to the third-and-a-half floor at school, my parents handed me a name and an address on a piece of paper, and told me I had to go to there after school and "talk to a woman." I was only eleven years old. By this point I knew what "talk to a woman" meant, although the idea of a psychiatrist or therapist still seemed remote. The first time I was supposed to go, I pretended I had the address wrong. I didn't. I just got off the bus and panicked. I crossed the street and got on the same bus, going in the other direction, and went home. As soon as I arrived there, the phone rang, and this very kind woman told me that we had had an appointment and asked me if I maybe had forgotten? I told her my planned-out story: "The paper said 630 West End Avenue, and that it was on 77th Street and I went to 77th, the numbers were in the 300s, so I didn't know what to do, so I went home." Although I had taken the liberty of indirectly diagnosing one or both of my parents with dyslexia (a little white lie!), I was quite pleased with my story and thought it was completely believable and clever. My parents didn't believe a word of it. They both looked straight at me and told me I lied.

Obviously, the doctor knew that too (she was a shrink after all!), but she asked me to come back the following week. Before she hung up, she made sure I had the correct address and phone number by asking me to repeat them to her exactly as I had written them.

The next Tuesday, in order to insure my arrival at the correct address, my father drove me to 360 West End Avenue and walked me inside the door. Thus began my first year in therapy. I was okay with my weekly therapy sessions, as long as they were never mentioned in front of my brother or my friends. Sadly, one winter afternoon, my cover was blown. I heard my father tell his assistant that he had to take me to *"the therapist."* His voice lowered in volume slightly on the last two words, and that is when I was struck dumb with the realization that I actually had a *therapist*, and not just an older friend to play games with because it might amuse me, which is what I suppose I had somehow convinced myself she was. My father's lowered decibel level on pronouncing the dreaded words further convinced me of their shamefulness. I felt my insides tighten, my stomach turn. I had been right all along: there was something terribly, horribly, deeply, irreversibly wrong with me.

The next year, when I was in fifth grade, my parents were called into school to talk to my homeroom teacher, along with the head of the middle school. A Chapin alum herself, who often wore a kilt that looked exactly like the upper school uniform, this particular woman was in every way the living embodiment of a WASP. I had always felt her look at me with vague disapproval, and I knew it was because she somehow didn't "get" me, or know what to do with me. According to these two women, my behavior in homeroom was incorrigible because my hair was always in my face, and I was not organized properly. According to my parents, these two women were full of shit and were suppressing my individuality, and, of course, "They just don't like you because you're Arab."

Had I been born ten years later, I might have been diagnosed with ADHD, given a pill, and sent on my merry way. Since it was only 1985, I was dismissed as disruptive, and because of my already deeply acute sense of self, I internalized the "diagnosis" I did get as being yet another symptom of my weird, ugly, dirty "otherness," and tried my best to behave in the appropriate manner for the rest of my tenure at that school.

IN MY HISTORY CLASS THAT YEAR, we each had to pick one of Napoleon's campaigns and do an oral report on it. Ever unsure of myself, I shyly asked my father to help me choose one. Ever himself, he picked one that we hadn't already studied in class, and one that no doubt brought "the Arabs" into my otherwise Eurocentric classroom. I felt my insides turn; the strands of anxiety that lived in my stomach came together in a big tangled mess as they so often did when I felt torn between my overwhelming but contradictory desires both to please my father by doing something he might be proud of and to blend in with the wall by doing an adequate job on my homework—certainly not one that was outstanding or unusual in any way. This was an *oral* report after all, not a homework assignment that only the teacher would see and grade, so I was inviting attention from my classmates. I imagined them smiling stiffly and saying, "That was really good," because they were such sweet girls and so polite, but really thinking, "Najla is really *so weird.*"

Ohhhh, why, why, why did I ask him? I chastised myself in my overactive head. At the same time, I smiled and nodded weakly, trying desperately not to show him my apprehension. Daddy, carried away by his excitement, passionately encouraged me, insisting I do it because it is "without a doubt the most interesting one, *and*"— he lowered his voice for a moment, and then raised it several decibels to make his point—*"the one that no one ever talks about!"*

"Why?" he continued rhetorically. "Because who cares about the Arabs, right, Naj?" I was getting more and more agitated and confused, but I held my breath and nodded.

"He went in there to try to gain control of the region,

because as I'm sure you know, the British controlled it, *and* he brought scientists! And all sorts of people, mathematicians! To 'study' the people and the culture! Can you believe it?"

I mumbled something about the Rosetta stone (wasn't that a good thing?) but he continued his lecture, "*And*, many believe that it was Napoleon who blew the nose off the Sphinx! With his cannon! Can you believe that? I can! It was an attempt to display and assert French imperial power! You didn't learn *that* in school, did you?"

We had studied ancient Egypt and we had all loved it. In art class, we had made sarcophagi out of clay and even put mummies inside them. I was captivated and thrilled by "ancient times." I had always been endlessly fascinated by inventions and how people created whole worlds from nothing. But Egypt (or Greece or Rome, for that matter) post ancient times had never been mentioned in fifth-grade history, or in any other class, and thus I was undeniably sure that if it were actually important to have learned about what Napoleon did there, we would have learned it. Still, I wanted so badly to please Daddy, and I was intrigued by what he told me about the Sphinx's nose. I knew no one in my class knew about that, and I bet they all had wondered about it. I considered: if it were indeed a true fact that I was able to discover in my research, I'd be considered a genius, maybe! I was not sure that even Mrs. Schroeder, our teacher, knew this fact! Otherwise, wouldn't she have taught it to us?

At this point, having piqued my interest and tickled my sense of rebelliousness, my father walked out of the room. He returned to his study and closed the door. I heard the clatter of the typewriter, and realized his work was done. Unfortunately, I had no idea where to begin.

❧

THE REST OF MY middle school career was, predictably, awkward. In that respect, I differed very little from every other eleven-to-fourteen-year-old on the planet. And though I was a late bloomer emotionally, I was not one physically. So, I was five feet seven inches by the age of twelve (I am still five-seven) and needed a bra in the seventh grade. Luckily, it was the '80s, so I could wear a baggy man's shirt and slouch my shoulders forward. My friends began to date, and some of the more advanced girls in my class even claimed to have had sex. I was starting to like boys, but only from far away. Two years earlier, I had begun taking after-school theater classes, which my parents thought might help me to open up a bit, and I continued all through school. Then, in 1984, an actress who was about my age appeared on a TV show called *Who's the Boss?* She had dark looks, and played a tough Italian girl from Brooklyn, but because her character's father had become the housekeeper of a wealthy WASP woman in Connecticut, her character grew up in a fancy part of what I believe was meant to be Fairfield County. Even though her character, Samantha, didn't fit in at first, ultimately she became just like everyone else at her school. She even became popular. The boys loved her and she looked pretty in everything. I actually hated the show ("It's sooooo cheesy") and thought the teenagers on it dressed really badly and "suburban," but I loved to watch it because it made me feel as if there was still hope for my acceptance in the world. I knew from *People* magazine that, like her character, Alyssa Milano was from one of the outer boroughs of New York City, and that when she was cast on the show her parents gave up their lives and moved with her to L.A., where she became a star. I thought that if she could do it, so could I. Thus began my quest to get my parents to make me into a child star. They pretty much ignored the whole thing.

But because this teen actress was Italian, and dark, and still accepted, I tried to find out if I might have some Italian in me. I repeatedly asked my parents about our ancestry and never once heard anything more than "We are Arab. Palestinian and Lebanese, that's all." I kept looking at the map.

"But, Mommy, Italy is close, right?"

"Well, yes, but Turkey is closer. And Syria."

Not wanting her to lose focus, I'd switch the subject back to Italy:

"But we might have an *Italian* relative somewhere, right? The Romans lived in Lebanon, didn't they? You said that, so we *could* be Italian, maybe, right?"

"Maybe."

"I have a great-great-uncle who married a Greek lady with a funny name," my father, hearing a bit of our conversation, chimed in.

"Greek isn't Italian, Daddy."

I went back to studying my globe, and dreamed of my imaginary Italian great-great-great-grandmother and her delicious spaghetti sauce.

A few months later, I heard my mother tell a story about a man she'd met who had the same last name we did, but was from Malta.

"What's *Malta*?" I asked, with obvious disdain in my voice.

"It's a country where they speak a mix of Arabic and Italian. It's a funny place, in my mind. Because the language they speak is so strange to my ears."

I jumped up and ran to my encyclopedia. I was absolutely completely thrilled. From then on, I would say I was *Maltese*!!! Unfortunately, I was far too shy to ever actually try this, but the possibility of it calmed me internally for a long time to come.

In the seventh grade, one of my best friends, Ashley, told me I was beautiful. To prove her point, she sketched my profile in her notebook when I wasn't looking. I stared at it blankly. I wanted to cry and laugh at the same time. I couldn't believe that a person I knew (that is, not a creepy man on the crosstown bus) had taken enough interest in my dark, strange face to want to draw it. I couldn't believe that in the eyes of this perfectly named, perfectly shaped, perfectly raised, perfectly dressed, perfectly perfect girl from the Upper East Side, I was beautiful. My confidence, for the first time since I was very small, began to grow that year, as I emerged on the other side of my awkwardness. By eighth grade, I felt comfortable telling my three closest friends, "My dad is Palestinian." He had been on TV a lot that year

(1988), explaining to Ted Koppel why Palestinian boys were throwing stones at Israeli tanks. One of my friends told me she'd seen him on *Nightline*, and another one said she had too. I suppose I quickly calculated that if they had seen him, they had also heard him, which meant that they knew he was Palestinian. And they were still my friends. I suddenly realized that Ashley would still think I was pretty and that Katie would still want to giggle and eat pizza with me after school, even when they found out that I was Arab, so I blurted it out, "I'm Palestinian and Lebanese," adding softly and encouragingly, really for no one's benefit but my own, "I can't help it, I was just born."

Though I said it only once before I left Chapin, I did say it, and it was a very big deal. I was beginning to grow into myself, and I almost trusted that my friends really loved me, no matter how weird my family was, no matter how different I seemed. And then I left. My parents had decided that I was going to leave my school and join Wadie at Trinity, which became coed in ninth grade, and I would have to make friends and find an identity all over again. Still, I had begun to ease into myself.

❧

ON THE BUS to a fall orientation trip for incoming students to Trinity, another new freshman invited me to come sleep over at her house that weekend, at the same time her family's "friends from Israel!" would be visiting. That was supposed to be an enticement. I was confused. I hadn't shied away from saying exactly where my parents were born, and this was the reaction. She didn't understand that for a Palestinian Lebanese American girl who had grown up in a world full of WASPs, and probably encountered approximately two Israelis in her life, hers wasn't the most appealing invitation. To me, it seemed as if she didn't want to accept that I was Arab, even though for once I had said it, and she had heard me. I imagined an awkward weekend with her family friends, which I knew would result in their having to explain to her patiently and carefully that I was evil and dirty. She would be mortified and disgusted at what she hadn't seen before, and I would feel as though I had misled her. I would apologize profusely and shamefully as she cast me out onto the street. So in the end, I thought it best to rebuff her kind offer. Fortunately, the girl next to her on that orientation bus ride kept talking to me, and eventually *she* became my best friend.

From the first days of our friendship, I marveled at how "cool" Jenny thought everything Arab was, how she knew how to eat all the foods we made, knew exactly what was going on in Palestine, how the Palestinians lived, what their *intifada* (uprising) was about. Jenny said things that I had only ever heard Arabs say, things like "Zionist propaganda" (until I met her I thought "Propaganda" was an Italian politician who drove my parents and cousins and uncles and aunts crazy) and "human rights violations" and "international law." Jenny had learned all this from a sister who was seven years her senior and was passionate about what was going on in the world. For the first time in my life, I wanted to know more. I also wanted Jenny in my house all the time. I had never had a friend that I knew my parents and brother would want to be friends with too; the thought of it thrilled me. Jenny would be my ticket to being taken seriously at home. It became a challenge for me to impress both my family and Jenny with what I knew about things, and I took every opportunity to ask questions of my parents in order to show off to Jenny later, and vice versa.

Jenny was from Brooklyn Heights, and her father owned his own business; he produced Passover food and health foods. Macaroons were his company's year-round best seller, and he named them after his Jenny. Arnold was the only father I'd ever met besides Jack, Catherine's dad, who neither *had to* wear a suit, nor chose to, like my own. He liked to go running in the cold and always seemed to be training for a marathon. He was just this casually dressed, no-bullshit kind of guy. I found him so refreshing. He ably oversaw all that went on at the factory he owned in Williamsburg, Brooklyn (which was not yet a place where hipsters or, later, rich kids masquerading as hipsters, lived) but adopted no pretensions despite his success and intelligence. Jenny's mother was similar. They were absolutely real in the best sense of the word; they reminded me of my own family, and made me feel safe and loved. They fought, laughed, teased, and slammed doors as much as the Saids did. There were papers, books, objects in their house; *things* were not hidden from view at all times to reveal a space that belonged in *Architectural Digest* or *Town & Country*. Though their house was tastefully and beautifully decorated, it was lived in, like my home. I felt welcome there and never once worried about ruining the wallpaper, or the rug, or the antiques, nor was I scared to sit on the couch for fear of creasing the cushions. For the first time since I had started kindergarten, nine years earlier, I felt at ease in a friend's home. And yes, it was the first really Jewish one I had ever been in.

Jenny, in turn, loved everything about my apartment. I had always been shy to invite friends over, embarrassed by our food, our furniture, my parents' language (whenever they spoke to each other in Arabic, I felt compelled to turn to whatever friend was around and translate nervously, so that she knew that they weren't talking about her or saying "terrorist" things), their culture, and their ways. Ordinarily, as soon as a friend walked into my family home, I would find things to apologize for. But I didn't have to open the door all the way before Jenny burst in with excitement. "Oh my God, I love it! I love the *smell* and the *books*, and, oh my God, the mahogany walls, it's *soooooo* Upper West Side! I hate my stupid Brooklyn house. You. Are. So. Lucky." I didn't know what Jenny meant by any of that, but since she obviously seemed happy, I breathed a sigh of relief. She loved the Upper West Side, she loved "intellectuals" and thought the older men with messy hair and overactive minds (who nonetheless probably couldn't figure out how to work a television) who populated my neighborhood and my home were "gorgeous" and "brilliant." In fact, Jenny was the first person to explain to me that my dad and brother were good-looking. I had no idea. She also had a massive crush on my cousin who, "Oh my God, goes to *Wesleyan*! *That's so cool.*" Maybe it was just during the brief period of time in which I grew up, but on TV, in all the movies, and even in the comic books I had read as a girl, the dark-haired guy was always, always the other, not-as-good-looking guy or "the bad guy" or "the dangerous rebel" (think Reggie, not Archie; Fonzie, not Richie, and so on). In short, the dark-haired, dark-eyed man would always get you into trouble. The WASP culture at Chapin did nothing but reinforce this idea.

Along with the highly intellectual conversation that was bandied about, Jenny loved the smell of the miles of books in our apartment, the smell of the spices my mom cooked with and of my dad's pipes, and she loved the classical music that he always blasted on the stereo. She was excited to hear my father play Wagner in the house, and said that her father did the same, "even though he's Jewish!" *Hannah and Her Sisters* was Jenny's favorite movie, and my parents' home, funnily enough, made her feel like she was in it. I began to see my family through an outsider's eyes, and the perspective was very different.

Jenny's older sister, Lisa, was living in Israel at the time. She was a fan of my dad's work and apparently spent as much time in the West Bank and East Jerusalem with Palestinian friends as she did in Israel proper with Jewish ones. As Jenny liked to constantly remind me: "You don't have to feel weird saying you're Arab around *me*; my sister fucked a Palestinian!" Jenny used words like "fuck" and "tit," words that made me cringe. I was so proper in ways I didn't even realize, and I couldn't believe some of the words that came out of her mouth. I would flinch as if I had been struck across the face when she used them casually; she made it seem as if she were saying "hat" or "box"! But in all truth, I loved her practiced nonchalance toward all things sexual.

Jenny was my gateway, and throughout high school I became more and more absorbed in the world of Jewish culture. By the time I finished high school, I was far more likely to say "Oy vey" and "I'm shvitzing" and a whole slew of other Yiddish words before I'd dare utter a word of Arabic, I'd kissed more Jewish boys than gentiles (all of whom made some comment about making peace in the Middle East by our actions), and I was constantly described as "the neurotic girl," or "the histrionic one," or "the hypochondriac." In fact, to this day, I've been called "a real-life Woody Allen character" more times than I'd care to mention, and sadly, every time I have insisted that no, actually I'm an Arab, it has been pretty much assumed that I'm just Sephardic.

And though my parents were fiercely proud of being Arabs, and very critical of Israel, there was something about being a native Upper West Side family that made us all seem partly Jewish. Most weekends, we went to Zabar's for cheese and cold cuts and bread and even lox and cream cheese, and then we picked up bagels from H&H, across the street. I wasn't the only one in my family who spoke Yiddish either. My mom had actually had a Hebrew tutor when I was little, because she was interested in learning the language that was so much like her own. She still often says things like "I am stressed because I have the whole mishpucha coming for dinner" and "This schmuck is kvetching about nothing. It's annoying me," all in her charming Lebanese lilt, which makes me laugh. My dad had a calendar of Jewish holidays he kept on the bulletin board in the kitchen, so he could keep track of when alternate-side-of-the-street parking was suspended. *"Happy Simchat Torah!"* he'd yell into the phone to a Jewish friend, who had no idea what he was talking about.

ᘉ

IN HIGH SCHOOL at Trinity I flourished. I looked like everyone else. I was smart. By the end of it all, I was even considered pretty. I had found my place. Finally. Except one time, emboldened by my new political awareness and acceptance of myself, I said something about Israelis that rubbed Jenny the wrong way. She angrily called me anti-Semitic, and I looked right at her and said: "I can't be anti-Semitic because I *am* a Semite. Both Jews and Arabs are Semites—you can look it up."

She got the dictionary. It said something like this: *a person who discriminates against or is prejudiced or hostile toward Jews.** I told her that that was the "connotation, and not the denotation of the word, and that our society is infected." I was mostly showing off some new words I'd learned that I was sure she didn't know the meaning of, but then Jenny threw the dictionary across the room. I didn't want her to hate me. I told her she was right, and we went back to gossiping.

---

* http://dictionary.reference.com/browse/anti+semite

It was in high school that I learned to use my dark looks (fine-tuned with much electrolysis, waxing, and a good pair of tweezers) and even my name to charm the boys I dated. "Big black eyes like a cow" became an asset. My name was one of the things that made me "exotic," "beautiful," and "mysterious." When I was younger and more awkward-looking, "weird" had been a more common adjective, but now that I was starting to look like a girl, and was in a school with pubescent boys, perceptions were different. I didn't complain, but I was definitely confused. One boy told me in eleventh grade: "You're the kind of girl I'd want to kiss with open eyes. I'd love to be devoured by your intense, deep, dark stare."

⁃

IN THE ELEVENTH GRADE, we studied Catullus in AP Latin. Latin was by far my favorite class in high school, and the poetry of Virgil, Catullus, and Horace was like little pieces of perfection to me. For some reason, I always struggled with English poetry, but Latin poetry to me was completely clear, moving, concise, and comprehensible. I'd stare at the page and wonder why this dead language written in random word order, and according to a meter that wasn't at all natural to my ears, made such *sense*. I could look at it and see the patterns, the word tricks, the ideas, the rhythm without even trying. I tried not to second-guess my understanding of such a notoriously difficult subject, but it was hard not to notice how much easier I found foreign languages than I did science, history, and math.

Catullus had written a bunch of poems to his girlfriend "Lesbia," which was a pseudonym for a real-life married woman named Clodia, with whom he'd had an affair. Clodia, our Latin teacher explained one day, tangentially, was known for her beauty and had been famously described by Cicero as "ox-eyed" or "cow-eyed," an exquisitely flattering epithet normally reserved for Juno, the goddess.

The class looked at me. I had always told people what my name meant, and had just recently started to try to convince people that "cow-eyed" meant "hot," but I wasn't entirely sure of my argument.

"*See??* I told you it's a compliment!" I grinned.

Our teacher concurred, and went into a long speech about the ancient obsession with "cow-eyed" women. I still resented my name, but at least I had proof that it was not totally weird to say "cow-eyed." If the people who invented the entire world a million years ago used it as a term of praise in their *poetry*, then maybe Arabs weren't so peculiar in their taste in women, after all.

I still got teased for my name after that, but the teasing also took on a new, pornographic sort of tone, and I was secure enough now to see that it was funny, not mocking.

"Hey, *méNajla trois*, what's up?"

"What does it take to get into the *Naj Mahal*?"

Yes, I am aware that these names are perfect examples of Orientalism, but to me it was a big step from "Snots-a-lot." It was attention—flattery—from boys, and to an insecure girl like me at the time, that mattered much more than any treatise my father might write.

I SET OUT TO FIND a way to exploit the "good" things about being Arab, to make myself at least *seem* as if I were beautiful, mysterious, and exotic, even if I privately knew otherwise. If eighth and ninth grades had been my horrible, ugly, awkward, and chubby years, I was determined for the remaining years of high school to fashion myself into the "beauty" that friends like Jenny insisted I was.

By this point, in the early '90s, my dad had become quite famous. It was impossible not to notice the way people acted around him and how they reacted to the fact that he was my father. Or was it that I now had a greater appreciation for his accomplishments? I no longer felt the embarrassment in my elegant, cosmopolitan parents that I had felt when I was younger. But that doesn't mean I was actually comfortable with my own Arab-ness.

There were still those moments like these in my life: The bus pass lady at school once said to me loudly, *"Your father is Gaddafi, right???"* I felt the long line of students behind me lean forward with curiosity, grabbed the pass from her, mumbled something corrective and apologetic, and walked away.

I was still a non-Zionist in a sea of Zionists. When Jenny asked me if it bothered me that her parents were Zionists, I said no, because it didn't. Then I went home and asked my parents what that actually meant. They explained that Zionism was a political movement that was exclusionary, inasmuch as it asserted that Israel retain its Jewish character, within at least parts of historic Palestine. I knew Jenny and her parents had been to Israel a handful of times and considered it a place for Jews, but that hadn't surprised me, or made me uncomfortable, because I also knew, very clearly, that her parents adored me, and had no cultural or racist misconceptions about Palestinians. In fact, they knew more about what was going on in Palestine than any other Jewish people I had ever met.

I knew that my parents were against violence in all its forms, and I knew that it wasn't fair that my dad was born in a place called Palestine that ultimately became a place called Israel. I didn't know it then but I believed in social justice and had been steeped in secular, humanistic thought since birth. I believed in the cause of a people that others quickly labeled "terrorists." This "cause" that I was attached to was definitely not something I thought of as in any way noble or just, though. In my adolescent consciousness, it was an embarrassing nuisance that made me different from my friends. I wished it weren't something I had to think about. I continued to wish that I were just "a quarter Irish, a quarter Scottish, a quarter German, and a quarter Swedish" like all my friends seemed to be.

When I entered high school, in the fall of 1988, the Palestinian intifada, which had begun a year earlier, was well under way. For a moment in history, images of young Arab boys throwing rocks at enormous Israeli army tanks became our sympathetic, albeit unintentional, calling card. Palestinians, while still in many ways a mystery to most Americans, seemed to be tugging at our collective heartstrings in much the same way that the Chinese man in Tiananmen Square and the young Germans who rejoiced as the Berlin Wall crumbled would.

My father was on television more and more. Many of my Jewish friends would see him on the news, and were at once impressed ("Your dad is so cool the way he shut down that Israeli guy by spitting out those facts and quoting those UN resolutions and totally not backing down") and unconverted ("I mean, I totally disagree with what he was saying, but, you know, I respect it. So frickin' cool, Naj"). I didn't care. I knew I believed whatever my dad said, and started to enjoy the notion that my family was somehow on the cutting edge of radical thought. I was just at the age when young people start exploring their own views, when "revolution" and "marijuana" become buzzwords; when, even if only temporarily, Che Guevara and Malcolm X begin to take the place of heroes like Abraham Lincoln and John F. Kennedy in the adolescent mind. I started to notice that my dad's status among those cool enough to know what was going on in the world was godlike. Jenny and her sister constantly confirmed this for me. Though I didn't want to be one of those people, those girls who smelled like patchouli and who went to rallies in Union Square on weekends and stuck to a strict vegan diet, I still thought they were cool, and was proud of the fact that they held my dad in such high esteem. I was vaguely fascinated by the idea of being committed and standing up for human rights, but the one protest I went to—an Amnesty International rally in solidarity with the protesters of Tiananmen Square—involved having to pee for a long time, being cold and hungry, and not really wanting to take the boring-looking leaflets the activists kept handing out to me. It all seemed too complicated to understand. I had wanted to go to that event because my friend Allison was going, and I wanted to hang out with her, but also because I wanted my dad to be impressed. He was, but was mostly amused and wondered why I didn't care about Palestinian rights and why I didn't make an effort to go to *those* protests. I rolled my eyes. "Daddy, *why* does everything have to be about *you?*" The world still seemed fragmentary to me, politics still seemed boring to me, and the Middle East was still a major pain in my butt. I got goose bumps and a lump in my throat when I heard my dad speak, I cried when I got to meet Nelson Mandela and when I saw footage of Palestinian kids throwing stones at tanks, but I didn't want to deal with those feelings. I had the choice to avoid it all, and I did.

When I was in the tenth grade and Wadie was a senior, our father was invited to speak at a school assembly. I was excited and proud, which was a huge step forward, but I still hoped he would talk about literature, and not politics. I did not need him to stir my friends into a state of outrage and debate over Middle Eastern politics. We often bonded over books and words and language and art, things we both loved, and I wanted him to amaze and inspire my friends and teachers with his brilliance. I was frustrated that no one knew him as anything but "a Palestinian." A few days before the lecture, I asked him what he was going to discuss.

"I think I am going to talk about *dissent*," he told me matter-of-factly.

"Oh, okay," I replied, and went back to whatever I was doing.

My father had used the word "dissent." I, however, heard "descent." I tried, for a good half an hour, to figure out what might be interesting and metaphorically brilliant about going down in an elevator, landing an airplane, or generational family relationships.

He came to the assembly and impressed everyone, including me. I don't think I listened to a word of his lecture because I was so nervous, but I did watch the students and teachers very carefully while he spoke. Of course, some students were flirting, talking, studying furtively, or simply sleeping, but most were riveted. I was so distracted by the larger implications of his being there that I have no idea what he spoke about. I do remember his discussing someone named I. F. Stone for a good long while, and I remember being relieved that whoever I. F. Stone might be, at least he had a normal name and wasn't involved in Palestinian politics.

At the end of his speech, Daddy took questions. One of the young teachers, just a year out of Yale, challenged him with the self-righteousness that only a twenty-three-year-old impressed with her own intelligence and good education could muster. He immediately shot her down, upending her argument and challenging her to rethink it in a more sophisticated way. Jenny bounced in her seat. This woman speaking up was her "cool" English teacher who talked about sex. Now she looked dumb! Jenny whispered:

"Oh my *God*, *Naj*, she is so stupid! She thinks she knows more than Edward Said!"

I smiled vaguely. Everyone cheered. Maybe no one understood what had happened exactly, but they did know that my dad had made a teacher look dumb, and that, to all of us, was nothing short of amazing. Jenny ran up to Daddy when it was over and squealed:

"Oh my God, you totally *dissed her*! That was so cool!"

My dad smiled and looked at me. He grabbed Jenny's upper arm and walked out of the chapel with us.

"Tell me, Jenny, was I really good? What does it mean that I 'dissed' her?"

I smiled as I walked with them. I was happy that he was happy. I was happy that Jenny was happy. For once, my two worlds seemed in sync.

Later that day, a girl in the class above me approached me:

"That was your *dad*? He is *so cool*! Oh my God. I am so inspired, ahhh! I can't even discuss it. It's amazing. *So cool*!"

Jenny smiled at me.

"See? I told you your parents were awesome."

For the next thirteen years of his life, my father tried to use the word "dis" in his everyday speech as often as he possibly could. My parents were cooler than I had thought, but they were still weird.

☙

WHEN THE GULF WAR BEGAN, in 1990, my eleventh-grade year, I started to feel less comfortable again. The incredibly long civil war in Lebanon had finally ended, and people stopped talking about Beirut as if it was the scariest place on earth. But now there was another war in another Middle Eastern country (one that had little to do with me!), and I could feel my new sense of safety and belonging beginning to slip.

Just before the invasion actually began, my friend Allison called me and insisted that we get coffee soon. She went to a different school so I saw her only occasionally, on weekends, when we made specific plans. She said we had to meet as soon as possible because of the impending war. She then went on to explain to me why our meeting was imperative: "Naji, Nostradamus predicted that in 1991 a city between two rivers would be destroyed, and we are about to go to war with Iraq, and New York, as you know, is a city between two rivers so, we have to hang out!!! Before we *die*, I mean!" Let me just state for the record that Allison is an extremely smart girl. But in the United States, when danger seems imminent, we panic, precisely because danger is never really imminent. We have no idea how to live through war and famine and political upheaval because we have never had to. Allison's reasoning seemed perfectly logical to me, and I was immediately convinced by her argument. I told my mom what Allison had said and expected her to react the way I had. With one deadpan sentence, my mother shot me down: "Baghdad is also a city between two rivers, Najla," she said, and began to walk away.

"Why do you people have to make everything about Arabs? Don't Americans count? Ever?" I shouted to her back.

She kept walking.

A few days later, I went to my friend Mike's house, to hang out after school. Mike and his family lived on Central Park West, about two blocks away from Trinity. His parents were "cool" (that is, they let us drink and smoke in their apartment). They were neither neglectful nor overly lenient, they were just "cool." This cold January day, I snuggled up on the sofa with some of my friends. We watched MTV and discussed things like Janet Jackson's abs, the strange, sudden proliferation of pop acts that were so awful it seemed like someone somewhere was trying to play a huge joke on the world (for example, Vanilla Ice, Gerardo,

Right Said Fred) and smoked cigarettes. Mike began to flip through the channels, and stopped on CNN when he saw that they were reporting live from Baghdad. Operation Desert Storm had finally begun that very week, and the chatter in the room hushed to silence as we all turned our attention to the live pictures from Iraq. The night was pitch-black, but every few moments a spark would "light up the night sky" (this was the phrase the commentators kept using). These so-called sparks were our American stealth bombs, which were not merely lighting up the sky as fireworks would, but landing on people's homes. The newscasters didn't mention that detail, though. They were talking about strategy and about Saddam Hussein, and about our weaponry and our defense tactics. My friends watched wide-eyed and spellbound. I shivered. I became antsy. "That is so, so cool," I heard someone say. The room remained silent; everyone seemed mesmerized. My eyes darted around. *What are they thinking? Why are they just sitting there?* My heart was pounding. I started crying but hid it well. I got up to leave.

"Naj, where are you going?"

"I can't watch this; it makes me sad."

"It's not *Beirut*! It's Baghdad! Come on!"

"That doesn't mean there aren't people on the other side of the bombs!"

"Yeah, I totally know what you mean, but Saddam Hussein is evil, and we are smart enough to have gotten most of the civilians out of the way . . . They're probably just bombing military targets! You're not from Iraq anyway; don't be so dramatic!"

"Yeah. You are right, totally," I lied. "Honestly, I am just really tired and I have so much work to do this weekend, and my SAT tutor comes in the morning so . . . I better go."

I left the party but was unable to shake the chills for the rest of the night. The phone kept ringing. It was PBS, it was *The New York Times*, it was Peter Jennings. He asked me if my dad was home and if I knew we had just gone to war. I said no to the first question and yes to the second (why did he think I was so dumb?) and went into my room. I got in my bed and pulled the covers over my head and turned off all the lights. I did this a lot in high school. No doubt it was partly for dramatic effect, but I also very often just wanted the world to go away. I would lie there in the dark, plug whatever music I was currently obsessed with into my ears, and stay there just long enough to forget what was going on in the outside world. Then, when I felt ready, when I had quelled the sense of isolation coursing through my veins, I'd reemerge carefully and set about doing my homework. I poured all my anxieties and fears into getting everything right, being perfect, getting straight A's. The more I felt my world spin out of control, the more I focused, with laser precision and thorough diligence, on getting everything else to be right.

At school, I ignored conversations that centered on the war. I didn't care about politics, I said, and walked away when discussions began. I did my homework instead and began to create schedules and charts for all aspects of my life. I did crossword puzzles obsessively; I focused on getting an answer for every math problem so that I could put a box around it and move on to the next thing.

The summer I was seventeen I went to France with a group of other students my age. We traveled as a group by train and bus, taking classes, hiking and biking through the Loire Valley, and staying with French families or in hostels or small hotels. Our group leaders encouraged us to communicate exclusively in French, even with one another, to blend in, so that we were seen as respectful, engaged visitors, and not bratty American tourists. For us, the trip was a chance to show the people who would be reading our college applications how diverse our life experiences had been and how serious we were about learning.

Because it was my first experience in Europe without

my family, I became aware of myself in a different way. Of course, as this was just after that first Iraq war, and because I was in France, the Arab-ness of my name was obvious to every French person I encountered, and as it began to very obviously intrude on my otherwise normal American identity, it made me want to disappear more than ever before.

We spent one week in Plouescat, a minuscule farming town in Brittany. Each of us was assigned to a job that week, and I was strangely excited to wake up on our first cold, rainy morning and set off with a couple of others to work on the shallot farm of Monsieur LeDouf. We got lost at first (apparently there was more than one Monsieur LeDouf with a shallot farm in this town of about twelve people) but ultimately found our way to work. It didn't take us long to realize that wearing plastic suits, kneeling in mud, cutting onions as the rain poured around us was not exactly glamorous. But at least, since the farmers were French, they took about seven lunch breaks before noon, bringing us with them into the back of a truck and plying us with red wine. In the afternoon, we returned to the fields and tried to make small talk with them. They were all much older than we were, some in their sixties and seventies, and they all seemed to have the same weathered faces, stocky builds, rosy cheeks, and jovial demeanor. At some point, one of the men began a conversation with his friend. He spoke rapidly and with great passion. I was barely able to make out the words, but I caught on quickly enough. He was complaining about a group of people who were "ruining" France. I leaned in to listen better. I lost track of the specifics after hearing him say *"les Arabes"* with disdain approximately ten times. He noticed I was straining to understand and, amused, tried to engage me in the conversation:

"Et toi, tu aimes les Arabes?" he asked me with a giggle, obviously aware that as an American I would have no idea what havoc *"les Arabes"* were wreaking on France.

I smiled sweetly, cocked my head, and replied in as singsongy a voice as I could, *"Eh . . . erm . . . je suis arabe, monsieur."* I followed that with a giggle of my own, for good measure.

He narrowed his eyes and looked at me with disbelief. He looked at his friend. They both seemed to think I was playing a joke on them. Nevertheless, my new friend continued to engage with me:

"Tu es arabe? Mais tu es américaine, n'est-ce pas?"

"Oui, mais ma mère est libanaise."

I said my mother was Lebanese because I knew the word *"libanaise"* (Lebanon, was, after all, a French colony) and I thought it would be simpler than getting into what a Palestinian was. His face broke out into an enormous grin, and he began to laugh, and nudged his friends to listen to what we were saying.

"Mais les Libanais," he corrected me, *"les Libanais ne sont*

pas arabes! Non, non, non, les Libanais parlent arabe mais ne sont pas arabes. Les Algériens, les Tunisiens, les Marocains— ces sont arabes! Non, en fait, les Libanais sont comme nous!"

He smiled at me approvingly, gave one more chortle at the absurdity of my assertion that I was indeed an Arab, and then told me it was time to go back to the truck to drink some wine together.

I felt weird for the rest of the week. I was happy that he realized that I was a "special, good" Arab, but I was also infuriated by his classification system. I was also appalled to realize that it wasn't just my young American friends who would accept me as somehow better than every other Arab in the world, but French people too! I didn't understand. I thought Europe, where I had always felt less strange, was a place I fit in. I knew that the French had been kicked out of Algeria and were not happy about it, but I thought that that whole thing was in the distant past. I assumed that since the French had lived among so many Arabs and in such close proximity to the Middle East, they would be more sophisticated in their approach to considering an entire race of people, but I realized as the summer went on that I was utterly wrong.

We went to Avignon and saw some plays that were part of the annual summer theater festival. One of the plays we saw was an adaptation of Albert Camus's novel *L'Étranger*. I had read it in my French class earlier that year, and had a visceral, pained reaction to the constant use of *"l'Arabe."* In fact, what I had felt in my gut in that class was something similar to what I had felt listening to the farm worker in Brittany.

Many of my fellow travelers had not read the book, and did not completely understand the French in the play. I probably would have had more trouble with it myself, but since I had suffered through the book, and had had the symbolism of the light and darkness, the alienation of the main character, drilled into my head by my French teacher, I was able to understand the whole thing, perhaps even more than I wanted to. The actors spoke Arabic and French; the very specific lighting and the Arabic-sounding music enhanced the mood and brought Camus's symbolic use of language into our experience. I was so moved by this production, I sat there mesmerized. My friends were giggling and talking. I wanted them to shut up. Something was happening to me, I was experiencing some deep level of comprehension that I couldn't quite articulate. Everything made sense but nothing was being explained. I was at once squirming in my skin and feeling a complete sense of understanding and being understood.

Later, on the phone, I tried to explain to my father that I had had this bizarre "aesthetic experience," and he seemed to understand what I meant, but still pressed me to analyze the words in the book; he stressed the importance of Camus's language and syntax. I understood what he was saying and appreciated it, but I also wanted to explain to him that it was *more than the words* that had affected me. I didn't know how. I gently tucked my overwhelming feelings back inside my gut and left the experience behind in France.

We concluded our six-week trip with a stay in the Alps. From Chamonix, we were ultimately driven to Zurich to catch our flight back home. When we arrived at the airport, we checked in, and were cleared through security. As the logic went, the worst thing a group of American teenagers with responsible adult chaperones could be carrying was pot, and our leaders had thoroughly checked and cleared our bags in advance, and we were all clear. We sat on the floor of the airport chattering and writing notes about how much we were going to miss one another and planning our reunion hang-out celebration in New York in a few months' time.

One of the airline representatives, an American woman with a ridiculously exaggerated smile that stuck out like a sore thumb in this European airport, approached us.

"Excuse me, kids. I need to speak to Miss Said. Is she here?"

I waved my hand tentatively. Everyone stared at me. Although this kind of thing had never really happened to me before, I knew why the lady was singling me out.

"Hi, sweetie, can you come with me for a minute?" she cooed.

"Yeah, okay, sure."

I smiled, and got up. I felt the twenty or so pairs of adolescent eyes that belonged to my trip-mates sting my back as I followed her to an arbitrary corner of the terminal, just out of earshot of my friends.

"Honey, I just have to ask you a few questions. It's no big deal, okay?"

"Sure," I said, trying to make sure I sounded as American as I possibly could, my face frozen in a perma-smile that mimicked her own. I noticed she was holding my passport.

"Okay. Where were you born?"

"Boston."

"Uh-huh, okay. And your mom was born where?"

"Beirut, Lebanon. But she's American."

"And your dad?"

"Jerusalem, he's American too."

I didn't say "Palestine" or "Israel" because I knew my dad had gone to great lengths to have the American Embassy amend his passport in this way. He got someone important on the phone and firmly but kindly explained that though he well understood that the city in which he was born was now, technically, part of the state of Israel, he himself was not born in a place called Israel. He argued that if they were not going to write "Jerusalem, Palestine" on the document, he would prefer that his place of birth remain one word: "Jerusalem." He got his way. I wanted to make sure I said exactly what each of my parents' official records said, so I wouldn't arouse any more suspicion. I was a good girl, I never did anything wrong, and neither did my parents. I had to make sure she saw that.

She smiled again, ticked some things off on a piece of paper, and released me. I felt so awful, so violated, so sick to my stomach, so embarrassed, I just sat down and cried. My friends were already making fun of the airline representative for being so strange and having the gall to think that I was in any way "dangerous." I felt as if the dirty, disgusting Arab me that I had buried so deep inside myself had been exposed for the third time in six weeks. My skin color, religion, and general appearance had helped to obscure my "true identity" for so long, I was only now experiencing the punch-in-the-stomach feeling of racism. It is very difficult to explain to people who know you and see you as "white" that you have been discriminated against because of your race. My friends convinced me that I was overreacting. They agreed that she had been mean, but said that it was probably a random search.

"You're so not Arab, Najla! You don't even look it!"

I felt so isolated from everyone else, I wanted to scream.

☙

AT THE END OF THAT SUMMER my parents told
Wadie and me that my dad had been diagnosed with chronic
lymphocytic leukemia. What they said was that Daddy had
leukemia, but then that it wasn't the kind of leukemia we
had seen in TV movies, in which the patient goes bald, is in
the hospital for ages, and either goes into remission or dies
quickly. It was, we were told, *chronic* leukemia, which was
less common and also less insidious than acute leukemia,
but that it was still going to kill him. It was going to take a
long time, and his treatments and illnesses would
be stretched out over many years, but Daddy had to "be
careful." His immune system was now compromised, and
he was ultimately going to die sooner rather than later.

The fear I felt was devastating. Inside, I still felt like a
five-year-old. I had barely gotten my footing in the world,
and now I felt I was slipping. I was confronting racism,
death, sex, and being on my own in the world for the first
time; it was too much, too fast. I felt so desperately out of
control of everything, I began to make major, life-changing
decisions in the span of one minute. I broke up with my serious boyfriend for no reason. My good grades suddenly
seemed to me to be "mistakes." I threw half my college applications in the garbage and kept only six arbitrary ones.

And then I made the brilliant decision to just stop eating. In truth, this was something I had been building toward since childhood and middle school, with my debilitating insecurities about my appearance and body size, but it was in high school, most markedly my junior and senior years, that I put actual starvation into successful practice. Having been in therapy my whole life, I can catalog for you the reasons why I became anorexic, starting with the annual height check/weigh-in at Chapin. Lining little girls up in alphabetical order, year after year, weighing and measuring them and then calling out the dreaded numbers for all to hear was probably not the smartest way to go about things at an all-girls school on the Upper East Side, but the main thing you need to know for now is that I stopped eating "anything with a gram of fat in it" (how very early '90s) somewhere between ninth and tenth grades. The fall of my senior year, when we found out about the leukemia, kicked my anorexia into high gear. None of this was conscious, of course, but in retrospect it's easy to see that I was so devastated by the fact that my daddy might die that I began to severely restrict what I ate, so much that I might die too. I wanted to take on his illness, and share it with him. I was depressed, and wanted to disappear. Anorexia, after all, is just a slow form of suicide.

Ironically, though, there was another aspect to it that was almost completely opposite: I knew from experience that being sick or "having a diagnosis" would get me noticed, and give me an identity (I was *sort of* popular, *sort of* pretty, *sort of* athletic, *sort of* smart, *sort of* good at art, and so on, but I *shone* at nothing). Wadie was a junior professional tennis player, and a boy, and the skinny one "who could eat anything and never get fat!" He was the funny one, the nonneurotic one, the one my mom worried about if he didn't come home by five p.m., and the one who was learning Arabic. Though the enviable word "exotic" had begun to replace the word "weird" as the main adjective people used to describe my difference, I was still not fully accepted as American, and if I were going to live up to being "exotic," I had to be perfectly so. So while I did not set out to be anorexic, per se, I did think that being described as "skinny" would be the best thing to ever happen to me. And after all, in the world in which I lived, wasn't that the best thing to be?

By the end of my high school tenure I was five feet seven inches and weighed 105 pounds. People noticed, but my parents insisted (to themselves more than anyone) that it was a phase that all teenagers go through, and that was that. In all fairness, my dad's sickness was a lot more daunting, unsettling, and immediate for them (and for me and Wadie as well); certainly, a discussion about the ramifications of my teenage diet could wait. I ate practically nothing, and organized my day around when and where I would do so. Popular girls envied me. People worried behind my back. I loved it. At the same time (such is the beast of anorexia nervosa), I continued to see a fat, hideous, unremarkable girl when I looked in the mirror. I knew my clothes were small, I knew I had lost inordinate amounts of weight, I knew I ate next to nothing and ran many miles a day, but I couldn't stop any of it.

☙

BY THE TIME we graduated from Trinity, in June of 1992, most of my high school friends had been to my "homeland" (which to them was Israel), but I still had not. Though I had spent most of my Beirut-exiled summers in the Hamptons and at summer camp like everyone else in my world, the all-important trip to Israel that my Jewish friends had taken with their families by then had eluded me.

Now Daddy, suddenly aware of his mortality, had resolved himself to return, with his wife and children, to the land in which he was born. It would be his first time back since he left permanently, in 1947. We were finally going to Israel as a family. But unlike the trips of my Jewish friends, this one would not be about the discos of Tel Aviv and planting trees and the Wailing Wall; it would be completely different.

Because I was going to Palestine.

DADDY HAD NOT BEEN BACK to the place of his birth in more than forty years. For him, the trip was clearly an important, emotional one. It was as if he ached to return at that particular time, with us, to come to terms with his own history and mortality, just as much as I ached not to. I understood that word—"ache"—quite deeply; my body ached constantly from the fatigue, the bones rubbing against bones as I tried to adjust the pillows in my sleep, as I struggled in my big black boots to lift my leg and walk, one step at a time, up a slight incline. My entire self ached from feeling empty, scared, lost, and rejected. "Rejected"—that was the only word I could ever come up with to describe my feelings: boys, colleges, life. Though I would be attending Princeton in the fall, all I could focus on was that I had failed to get into Harvard, which was the school my father had wanted for me. I did not think I was enough. The trip made it all so much worse.

Forced to go on a family vacation at a time when I was supposed to be independent and having fun with my friends, I sulked dramatically and sighed with boredom at every conversation about our upcoming trip.

Meanwhile, Wadie, now a sophomore at Princeton, seemed to embrace and understand his identity more each year. He had grown into a brilliant young man. In high school, it had seemed to me that while I agonized over my schoolwork and put in hours upon hours of effort, Wadie was able to play tennis every single day, watch basketball, play video games, talk on the phone, and still get excellent grades and gain early admission to Princeton. Moreover, he had completely transformed himself from a typical American teenager into a charming, serious student of Arabic language and culture. I was convinced, when this transformation occurred at the beginning of his college tenure, that Wadie had planned it just to piss me off. It felt as though he had completely betrayed me. He had joined my parents comfortably straddling the line between "East" and "West," and had left me standing alone and lost, in America.

He was also, I am not going to lie to you, the son in an Arab family, and no matter how unconventional and mixed-up we were, I knew that for my dad the return to Palestine was a lot more about him and my brother bonding than it was about me and my edification. Sure, my daddy adored me, but I was kind of like his little doll. Little girls like me didn't need to know about serious things; that was the message I received. And it was one of the reasons I hadn't felt more motivated to learn about my culture. Wadie, the son, was going to carry on our name; why should "little Naj" be burdened with the knowledge of her history? This was clearly the family's thinking, and for much too long, I accepted it.

And so, age eighteen, petulant, and on my way to Palestine, all I could think about was being stuck for three weeks in close quarters with this motley crew of overly excitable, weirdly political characters known as my family members. Who the *hell* was I going to talk to? What the *hell* was I going to eat?

We landed in Tel Aviv and I felt my insides turn. I was convinced that everyone was staring at us. I was certain we would end up in jail for trespassing on Israel. Everything went smoothly at customs; we were met by an Arab member of the Knesset (Israel's parliament), who made sure we were treated well. But when we got our baggage, Daddy's suitcase was missing. We reported it to the airport, who said it was lost but seemed to know exactly when they would find it. They gave us an address where we were to pick it up, in exactly two days' time, at a specific time. Daddy became agitated.

The heat was suffocating. As we drove to our hotel, I stared out the window at the landscape and waited to feel something amazing, but in truth, I was in no state of mind and body to feel anything close. Had amazing looked me in the face, I don't think I could have recognized it.

There it was, speeding by my window: the Promised

Land. It looked to me like nothing but a horrifically frightening place. There was greenery, but I noticed only shrubs. There was water, but I noticed only desert. And everywhere that there was a small Arab town it seemed to be surrounded by concrete slabs of unmovable earth. These, I learned, were the "settlements."

We set about exploring the country the very next morning. In spite of its proximity to my mother's native land, this place did not seem at all like Lebanon. Despite the war, Lebanon still flourished in my heart, but here I saw only division, separation. Going to Palestine knowing you are one of "them" but looking, sounding, and acting like one of "us" was just confusing. The Arabs spoke to me in Hebrew, or Italian, or Spanish, but never Arabic, and I smiled awkwardly, unsure of how to explain myself.

There was a cheeky British photographer, Gavin, following us around for our entire stay. He had been hired to capture our experience in sepia tones for the London *Observer* article my dad was writing about the trip. Mostly, he got in the way. To me, the bizarre, constant presence of Gavin the photographer made our supposedly meaningful trip seem like a farce, a reality show from a time before they existed. Every shot he took was calculated, prepared:

"Can you notice that old tree for the first time again? So I can get a shot?" he said to my father.

"Can you stand next to that Hasidic man so it's ironic? Cool. Yeah.

"Can you show your kids that plaque??? But yeah, um, let's not actually have them in the picture though. Can you guys move, please, so I can get your dad?"

Gavin's stupid flak jacket seemed ridiculously out of place as well, as if meant for some more exciting assignment he wished he were on. His presence made the whole event seem absurd and actually highlighted the fact that we were outsiders; we didn't have to live here, we could visit and document our "experience."

Every time we were in the hotel together as a family, my father was intercepted for an interview. There were journalists everywhere. It was quite surreal. On the one hand it was this "homecoming," a "family trip," and on the other hand it was completely transparent and contrived.

The anorexia really took over on this trip. I ate lentil soup and fruit for dinner every night at the hotel. That is all I ate every day. We kept going to people's houses for lunch and I would not eat. In Arab culture, this is the ultimate insult—refusing food.

"She's a vegetarian," my mother would politely say on my behalf, as I pursed my lips and stared in horror at my plate. Her excuse worked for a few days' pass, but then word got out that "the doc-*tor's* daughter doesn't eat meat." From then on, everywhere we went, there were *heaping* platters of rice and vegetables just for me. I still refused it.

The hotel we stayed at was the American Colony, to my initial great relief (an "American" hotel seemed more likely to have a gym, skim milk, and clean rooms). It was situated in the middle of Arab East Jerusalem, and was teeming with journalists and photographers. This was the hotel they all stayed at to be closer to the action, I supposed. Indeed, there were very few other tourists staying there. I should clarify that statement: there were, ironically, very few *American* tourists at the American Colony Hotel. Those tourists were all in West Jerusalem, on the other side of the same city, visiting Israel.

Though we were staying in Arab East Jerusalem, it was West Jerusalem in which my father was born. At that time, of course, there was no "West" and "East," but, well, now there is, and so we are from what is now, technically, Israel.

And so, when we ventured to my father's childhood home, we were heading into the belly of the beast. Lots of prime ministers and defense ministers and other kinds of ministers inhabit the huge houses in well-kept Talbiya, the neighborhood of my daddy's youth.

We walked around in circles until we found the house. Daddy was filled with panic and nervous energy; he was unsure of how he might react on seeing his house again after so many years, but he knew it would not be lightly. I did not want to see my father cry, as I had at his mother's funeral two years earlier. It had pained me more than anything I could have imagined. I also had the same very paranoid feeling I'd had when we landed at the airport. I couldn't help but feel as though someone in the neighborhood was going to lean out of the window, see us, and call the police to arrest us for being Arabs. On top of all of that, both my brother and I were obsessed with the possibility that the plaque on the door of the house of my grandparents—which is still technically ours, mind you— would bear the last name of one of our best Jewish friends from New York.

Thankfully, we were spared that. Instead, however, on the door of the house we had seen so many times in my grandfather's Super 8 films, we were confronted with a plate that read, in great big letters: "The International Christian Embassy."

MY FATHER LATER clarified in his *Observer* article, after researching the organization, that this rather benevolent-sounding society was, in fact, "a right-wing fundamentalist Christian and militantly pro-Zionist group, run by a South African Boer, no less!" As we are Palestinian Christians, the irony was not lost on us.

☙

DADDY AND HIS immediate family were not *actually* forced out of the house by Israelis in 1948, but rather had left in 1947 and taken up permanent residence in their second home, in Cairo. But though the family was lucky enough to not see their village burned, their town renamed, and their passports rendered useless; though they didn't end up in a refugee camp in Palestine, Jordan, or Lebanon, with only an identity card and no basic rights, nonetheless, their home was taken, along with all of their possessions, and they were exiled, never to be allowed back as anything but visitors. And the privilege of being a visitor was bestowed on them thanks only to the American citizenship my grandfather had passed on to them as a result of the many years he had spent in the States.

My father circled the house feverishly with my camera, shooting picture after picture of the façade. He remembered the park that was across the street, now beautifully manicured and filled with nannies playing with their small Israeli charges. He recalled the porch, the gate. Daddy even pointed up to the window of the room in which he was born. After every realization, exclamation, and configuration of a memory in his head, he ran his hand through his hair like a child who was trying to remember where, on the long road he had traveled, he had lost his way.

And he resolutely refused to go inside, as if entering would confirm the reality of what had happened.

We walked the narrow streets of the old city of Jerusalem. We visited the Arab towns of Hebron, Bethlehem, Nablus, Nazareth. There were Israeli soldiers everywhere we went, on the side of every street, outside every tourist site. I would constantly look around to find a face that understood me, that recognized me as someone who belonged there. I found comfort nowhere but in the faces of the Palestinian children we met along the way. They, like me, were silent. They very clearly had no control over their surroundings. They were simply born into this history, and just like me, they had no memories of a Palestine other than the one in which they lived. But unlike me, they knew no other outside world, and in their ignorance of another reality, they seemed so sweet, so innocent, so playful, so normal.

And yet, I realized, they were the ones who would suffer on a daily basis in a way that I never would. They were victims of the circumstances of their birth in a way that I would never be. And they were the ones who would have to deal, not just mentally, but actually, for the rest of their lives, with the consequences of a history that they, like me, might never fully understand.

Though I didn't encounter as many of them, I realized that the Israeli kids were stuck in a similar trap. None of us had emigrated or immigrated or fought in wars or suffered the Holocaust, but we still were the ones who had to bear the burdens of our peoples' respective histories.

It was on this trip that I learned that my parents both grew up in Arab cities with Jewish quarters that were as much a part of the city as any other neighborhood. In the Beirut of my mother's youth, there was not only a Sunni Muslim area, a Shiite area, and a Christian area, there was also a Jewish area. (Even now, after more than one Israeli invasion and countless internal religious battles, the synagogue still stands in Beirut.) And as in any other big city, each quarter earned its particular designation because of the families who settled there, and not because someone drew a line.

My mom told me the story of how her famously philanthropic mother had put money "for the Jewish home" in a blue box on the coffee table of a German Jewish neighbor in Beirut, without knowing that that "home" was going to be in Palestine. My dad talked of his Jewish friends in Egypt. My mom reminded me that her school, the one her mother ran, was in the Jewish quarter of Beirut. I wondered how their experiences were different from mine.

I considered the Israeli kids in the park with their nannies. Their parents and grandparents might have been victims of the *European* Holocaust, but those same adults probably never thought anything about Arabs until they got to Israel. Yet here, now, not so much later, their children— me, these kids—none of *us* had ever known the other as anything but an enemy.

It seemed so bizarre. I was suddenly struck by the reality of this conflict. It had *not* been going on for centuries. Its origins were recent; long ago and at the same time not so long ago. Each group of children has the memories of our parents' separate tragedies to defend and protect, and none of us really get it.

The divisions and separations began to suddenly multiply spasmodically in my head, and then collide and violently come together—Palestinian, Israeli, Arab Christian, Arab Muslim, Arab Jew, Palestinian American, Jewish American.

My father stopped in his tracks on the way back to the car to tell me what he really thought about the Middle Eastern conflict:

"Naj, you know, it's my generation that's messed it all up; we are too connected to the events of '48 and '67. We were there, we participated . . . and until we're all gone— my generation, the Sharons and Arafats and all of us— nothing's going to get done. It's up to your generation to fix it, really."

He put his arm around me as we resumed our walk. I

turned my head to stare back at the saucer-eyed Palestinian children whose blank expressions mirrored my own.

I began to photograph them obsessively, wherever we went. I had no other way of capturing what I felt inside.

❦

ON TUESDAY, June 16, 1992, we piled into a UN vehicle and went to Gaza. My mom had told me I had to wear a skirt that day, which I initially thought would be no big deal, since I had brought many with me on the trip. As I got up from the breakfast room to change, my mother quickly and apologetically added that it could not be a very short skirt, though. I was taken aback for a moment, because my mother never seemed to care what we wore, but I heeded her warning and carefully chose a blue crepe agnès b. skirt that my parents had given me for my birthday. "Long" by my standards at the time, it hung just *above* my knees. I put on a pair of brown suede oxford shoes from Fratelli Rossetti, an elegant store on Madison Avenue. I had no idea what was expected. I had no idea what to expect. I thought I looked modest enough, especially since my rail-thin body and baby face made me look much, much younger than my eighteen years, but as soon as we entered the van, the driver suggested he stop for me and my mother to get us some sort of full-length abayas (cloaks) and hijabs (headscarves) on the way. My mother refused, chiding the driver in Arabic: "We are not Muslim. But we *are* Arabs, and we can be respectful without being covered head to toe."

He nodded his head, and let us be. I wanted to throw up.

We entered the Strip through a military checkpoint. There were army posts and intimidating soldiers manning stations all over the area, and more barbed wire than I have ever seen. Daddy commented to us (and later in his article) that the entrance gave the place "the appearance of an enormous concentration camp."

We were searched, cleared, and let through.

I took pictures from the car window as we approached Gaza's Jabaliya Refugee Camp. There were people everywhere.

"This place has the highest population density in the world," Daddy told us. "Sixty-five thousand people live here on top of each other—Naj, are you listening?—in half a square mile of space!"

I was listening, but I didn't need to hear the details. I could see everything. The car windows were closed, but I could still smell the open sewers. Daddy continued to lecture us, all the while mentally taking notes for his article:

"The statistics are nightmarish: terrible infant-mortality

rates, high unemployment, the lowest per capita income in the Occupied Territories, the most days of curfew, the fewest medical services, and on and on."

And this was twenty years ago. Gaza today is much, much worse.

❦

DESPITE MY MOTHER'S insistence that my outfit was fine, I felt very conspicuous and alienated from "my people" as I descended from the car. Then I put my fancy suede shoe down into the muddy earth of Gaza and inhaled that horrifying *stench* of raw sewage; it had penetrated the car window, but I had really only faintly smelled it when I was inside the vehicle. At that moment, I truly realized that I had absolutely no idea. About anything.

We had lunch at the house of some "important" people. As we entered, all of the men, including my brother and father, were guided into one room, the women into another. I was confused. I had been to the Middle East many times before, and despite my relative isolation in recent years, had nevertheless grown up around lots of Arabs, Muslim and Christian alike, yet this was a custom that I had never encountered anywhere but in the movies.

I followed my mom into the female salon. The women

began talking about cooking. I understood them, of course, but my Arabic was too weak for me to respond. Frankly, though, I really had nothing to say. I didn't cook; I didn't even eat! My mother nodded, smiled, and politely answered all their questions. I could tell she was slightly bored but was making every effort not to show it. I too was bored, so I slipped away into the room with the men. A saucy, defiant act it was, but I knew I would get away with it. I knew that to these people, I was both "just a little girl" and an essentially American one; I could always pretend I didn't know any better.

My father saw me in the doorway and waved his hand, gesturing for me to come in. Quite a few of the men jumped up to give me their chairs, but I smiled sweetly and quietly perched myself on the arm of my father's, where I ultimately drifted off into a daydream. They were, much to my chagrin but not to my surprise, talking about what men in the Middle East *always* seem to be talking about—politics. I felt like I had played the part of the bored teenager in this scene in just about every country in the Arab world, so I knew what to do: tune out. Arab men always, always seemed to want to sit and talk, very seriously, about politics! They would all listen intently to one another, everyone would smoke a lot of cigarettes, drink cups and cups of Arabic coffee, and some would finger prayer beads as they thoughtfully considered the argument to which they were giving audience.

In this smoke-filled room in Gaza, all eyes were fixed on my dad. Most of the men did not even know why my father was important, other than that he was a connection to the outside world or, more specifically, the West. The irony of my dad's renown is that, until he passed away, his face and his name were far more familiar to people outside Palestine than they were to anyone who actually lived there. They did know he was important, though, and that they had been brought here to tell him their stories.

After we left, I asked Daddy to explain to me exactly what had been said (I wouldn't have been able to follow the heavily accented Arabic conversation even if I had been listening). Later, in his article, he used virtually the same words he had used with me:

I didn't hear a single hopeful thing in the two hours I was with the men. One of them spoke of having spent seventeen years in jail, of his children sick, of relatives destitute. There was a lot of anger. The phrase I kept hearing was "mawt batiq," slow death. There seemed to be considerable animus against West Bankers, who were variously characterized by Gazans as spoiled, or privileged, or insensitive. We are forgotten, they all said, and because of the unimaginably difficult job of dramati-

cally (or even slightly) improving the general lot of Ga-
zans, I was repeatedly enjoined at least not to forget.

I can try to conjure a picture of Gaza, but all I really remember of that day is a feeling. There was a dead goat (head and all) on a platter for lunch and there was a small piece of fruit given to me by one of the young girls at the house, which I pretended to bite into, and chew, and swallow. She had plucked it off a tree near the porch for me, and then chose a second one for herself. She popped hers into her mouth and smiled. All that I noticed was the layer of filthy dust that covered the one she had given me. I didn't want to eat it because of the (eight?) calories, but I also wondered how anyone could eat any piece of fruit without washing it.

The inside of the house was immaculate and beautifully decorated, even though outside was stinky and dirty. I tried to wrap my teenage head around the existence of such a place in the world, where people are trapped like caged animals in the filthiest zoo on earth, while I somehow got to prance around in suede shoes and $150 skirts and then get on a plane and go home.

In this way, the trip to Palestine added yet another dimension to my anorexia: I wanted desperately to suffer, not just for my daddy but for all of Palestine as well. I felt guilty, horrible, and sick to my stomach. I never wanted to eat again. How could I, when others who were just like me in every other way were unlucky enough to be born into nothing?

My need to feel real pain and suffering intensified on the drive back to Jerusalem. I turned on my Walkman, and I played one song over and over and over. Piama, one of my best friends, had put it on a mixtape for me. I didn't know where she'd found it; it was just a song on an EP by an unknown artist (Piama and her twin sister, Alex, always seemed to discover everything before anyone else). Regardless, it was in the car ride back from my day in Gaza that I really heard it for the first time. It seemed to speak to every single inexpressible thing I was feeling inside me at that moment: all of my teenage angst, my desire to share in my father's suffering from cancer, and now, my intense need to feel the pain of these people. The sun set as we drove back through the desert, and looking back it seems so poetic to me: there I was, in the land of "our Lord and Savior" and I actually wanted to become some sort of ascetic, crucified, suffering martyr. I wanted to stop being so conspicuous, I wanted to go away, I wanted to scream loudly, *"Why is all this happening?"* but I had no voice. My body had become my voice. Starvation, more than ever, would become my language.

And Tori Amos sang "Why do we crucify ourselves" in my ears, until I was gasping for air, still trying not to cry.

A million thoughts began racing through my head. I wanted to know why I was born lucky; I wanted to severely punish myself for being born lucky. Why didn't I have to live here? Why was I able to pass as a Jew if I wanted? Why did I get to go to the best schools in the world? And why, despite all this, did I still feel awful?

We finally left Palestine for Jordan. The short but tense and usually harrowing journey across the Allenby Bridge is experienced daily by many Arabs, who know that, depending on the day, on the mood of the soldier who holds the exit or entry stamp, or on the current political climate, they may not make it either in or out of Israel, and if they do, it will not be without a long wait, a lot of questioning, searching, and humiliation. The day we crossed over, we would be joining them. But just as they had at the airport in Tel Aviv, our American passports made our journey across the Jordan River a much less scary one. Nevertheless, we did have to wait for almost two hours, and as I sat, reading my book, Israeli soldiers, who were more or less my age, sat beside me and tried to get my attention. Even though their thoughts were amorous ones, I felt so frightened, so scared, I could barely move.

My mother told me later it was my own fault:

"*Tayb*, Najla? Why is the top you chose to wear formfitting? Why were you blowing bubbles with your gum? And why was the book you chose to read *Lolita*?"

Once we were across the bridge and into Jordan, the fences around all of our hearts melted. There was a huge collective sigh of relief, and my mom burst into nervous laughter as she noticed the sign on the road that read:

YOU ARE IN JORDAN. SMILE.

The Jordan branch of the trip was relatively unexciting, especially compared to the previous few days. My father's extended family had settled there after 1948 (as had many other Palestinians), and hanging out in Amman seemed more like hanging out in a suburb in America than it did like being roughly sixty miles from Palestine.

Everyone in my family had an American accent, went to an American school, lived in a big house with video games and VCRs, and drove some sort of an SUV. We attended two over-the-top family weddings and stayed in an enormous fancy hotel. As we drove around the city, Omar Sharif, my father's former schoolmate from Egypt, smiled down at us from the billboards advertising his eponymous cigarettes, which, the sign told us, "are very soft, smooth, and sensual, just like my romantic life." Palestine, though just a few miles away, was gone. And with it went the barbed wire, the fear, and the sadness.

While we were in Amman, my father took us all to the palace of another former schoolmate, King Hussein, where he had to pay a visit to Yasir Arafat. Two months earlier, Arafat's private plane had crashed in the Libyan Desert, and after a momentary death scare and some ambivalence on the part of the U.S. government to help rescue him, the wreckage of the plane was found—Arafat still alive. It was for this reason that my father felt we ought to pay him a visit, even though Daddy and the PLO chairman had very different ideas about Palestine. Arafat was someone Daddy knew who had been in a scary accident and it was the right thing to do to visit. Propriety won over in this instance.

As we entered the palace, however, I immediately felt as though we were stepping back into the austere reality of Palestine. Arafat kissed me heartily on each cheek, and I wiped my hand across my face in disgust. Daddy had often asked me why I disliked Arafat so much, since he was "the only leader we have." I am sure he suspected it was because I just wanted to hate anything about Palestine, but when I told him, honestly, "When I look at him the way Americans do, he looks like a stupid idiot," Daddy laughed. He had never been a big fan himself, but thought he ought to support the person who was the figurehead of the cause he championed. He always acted civil and respectful, but, I noticed, he couldn't help but smile as I wiped Arafat's slobbery kisses off my face without even pretending to be deferential in the company of a world leader. Tradition and good manners called for respect, and Daddy behaved accordingly, as did my mother and my brother, and the rest of the men in the room—well, as usual there were *only* men in the room, except for me and my mom. I don't think anything happened at this meeting. We sat there. The TV was on. The sound was off. Everyone smoked. No one said anything. And then we left. (Clearly this is why nothing *ever* gets accomplished in the Middle East.)

FINALLY, WE LEFT JORDAN for our final destination: Lebanon. The war had ended just two years earlier, in 1990, and while I knew intellectually that things would be different, that life in Beirut would be a little less idyllic than I recalled, I was so thrilled at the possibility of maybe feeling at home somewhere in the Middle East, I could not contain my excitement. As the plane touched ground, my heart bounced and my stomach flipped. I looked out the window and wanted to cry. Applause erupted in the cabin as it always had before, and I did not see smoke or hear bombs. I was relieved. But the ride to our apartment was sobering, and the realities I saw during the rest of our stay in Beirut saddened and disappointed me in a way I could never have imagined. Part of my disappointment was standard: everything that had seemed huge to my childhood eyes was now remarkably small—my grandfather's garden (Where were the miles of grass? Was it always only about a hundred square feet?), the streets of Beirut (Was Teta Hilda's apartment really only one block away from Jiddo's? It was such a long walk before, why was it suddenly nothing?)—but part of my disappointment was unique, and steeped in horror, because everything that hadn't simply shrunk was gone, bullet-ridden, or frozen in time. I said something to my cousin about *Great Expectations* and the misery of coming home to Miss Havisham's cobweb-ridden house. He pressed me to try to look again. Then somehow, partly because of my recent trip to the living nightmare that was Gaza, and partly because I made an effort to notice how the Lebanese perceived the things that saddened me, I did begin to notice my surroundings in a more positive way. There were blossoming gardens on every balcony, ripe fruits and vegetables on every table, and there was laughter everywhere. On the outside it was naturally a little more depressing: what was most apparent and unavoidable were the massive shelled-out skeletons of what were once majestic buildings. But there was also ebullient evidence of life: restaurants, bars, and stores, of course, and in true Lebanese style, everyone was at the beach enjoying the summer weather.

I asked my mother if it made her sad to see the city she knew as a child this way, and she said, "Yes, but that's life. They will rebuild it, you'll see. You don't know the Lebanese like I do." I did not yet fully comprehend what she meant by that, but I was starting to catch on.

Three long, hot, dusty weeks after first touching down in Tel Aviv, we returned home to New York. Our journey could not have ended without a special, truly Middle Eastern experience: a thorough search at the Beirut airport, during which I was frisked aggressively by a female officer. The rest of my family was off getting searched themselves, so there was no one there to help me explain to this woman that there was *nothing* dangerous under my dress. She was extremely suspicious of a hard object under my clothing and repeatedly pounded her hand against it. It was just my hip bone, jutting out in all its emaciated glory, but as I didn't know the Arabic word for "hip bone," and was certainly not going to say "I'm very, very, very, very skinny" (because *clearly* I was fat), I stumbled and stammered, trying to explain. She became even more suspicious, and ultimately brought me behind a curtain. At her bidding, I cringed, took a deep breath, and lifted up my dress, much more horrified and fearful of the fact that she was staring at my "rolls of fat" than of any suspicion that I might indeed be packing heat.

One night that August, just before I left for college, I was suddenly overcome with a terror that I couldn't shake: there was something wrong with my brain and I needed to fix it or I'd die. That's what I said to my dad when I walked into the living room five minutes later and collapsed in a heap of tears in front of his chair. He looked up from his book. I was wearing a very thin nightgown and my bones were poking out. He looked at me carefully and saw the terror in my eyes. His own eyes flickered with a sense of concern, confusion, and fear. He asked me to explain slowly what I was trying to say. Originally, my parents and brother had thought my diet fixation was "a teenage girl thing" that I'd outgrow, but after our trip, my weight continued to drop, along with my mood, and they had all started to look at me with horror. And yet they didn't know what to do or say. I looked up at my father from the floor, where I sat hugging my knees to my chest, tears streaming down my face, and said calmly, "Daddy. There is something very wrong with my brain."

The next week they sent me back to the shrink I hadn't seen since I was fourteen. He knew after five minutes of talking to me that I had what I knew I had: *anorexia nervosa*. The rest of the scenario played out like it would in an after-school special. He sent me with my parents to the best-known doctor in Adolescent Medicine in New York City, Dr. Andrea Marks. She examined me, weighed me, and asked about the tufts of fur on my back and arms. "I'm just Arab," I said, dismissing the assumption that the hair had grown there to keep me warm (for once, I knew that "being Arab" could possibly work in my favor). She looked at me skeptically, gently put a hand on my back, and asked me to please dress. For a moment I was deeply moved; she had the most sincerely loving and caring expression on her face.

Dr. Marks advised my parents not to send me to Princeton in a few weeks as planned, but to the hospital instead. Their faces froze in confusion. They desperately wanted to believe I was still normal, and were half hoping that a little pill or something would fix me. They looked at her pleadingly. I insisted I should be allowed to go to school; I'd get better. (I didn't want to disappoint my parents.) Dr. Marks finally exhaled a breath and agreed to let me do outpatient therapy, if I could gain a pound a week until I left for school. Then, she said, if I continued to gain one pound a week while there, and if I agreed to come into the city every week, sometimes twice, to see her and to see the shrink, I could go. I agreed.

When we got home, my parents continued to act out the TV movie I wished I was watching, asking me repeatedly how they had failed me, why I wanted to hurt them, hadn't they given me everything? And, perversely, for the first time in a long time, I felt acknowledged.

MOMMY AND DADDY helped me load my bags of clothing, my CDs, my stereo, my three cases of Ensure Plus into the car, and drove me to Princeton to begin my freshman orientation. Wadie, a junior, was there already; he had arrived early for varsity tennis practice. My cousins Ussama and Kamal would be there as well, in graduate school. I would be living less than an hour and a half from home; I'd be traveling to the city every week for my doctor's appointments. I had already spent months away from home at camp, even as a young child, but something about going to college felt worse than anything I had ever felt, because I knew that from now on, I was completely on my own. And I didn't know how to take care of myself. I couldn't even eat without consulting a piece of paper written on by the doctor, and I felt as though I had nothing to look forward to but the further disintegration of my precious nuclear family and the death of my father.

I held Daddy's hand as we walked around the outside area of Forbes College, where I would be living for two years. The college had once been the Princeton Inn, and Daddy told me about how his parents had stayed there when they came with him to Princeton *his* freshman year. The lump in my throat grew bigger. I gripped his hand fiercely. I hated imagining him all alone, more than five thousand miles from Egypt, where his family was, with only letters as a means of communication until he could get on the boat and go back home to see them the following summer. I felt guilty about being so scared as he told me how lucky I was to have the opportunity to study here, and how envious he was of all the reading and learning I would be doing for the next four years. We went back to my room. Mommy, having returned from making Wadie's bed, began to make mine. My roommate appeared. A kind, shy blonde from Shawnee, Oklahoma, Lauren seemed the exact opposite of me. She had fair hair and blue eyes, was very petite and demure, spoke slowly and respectfully, and smiled a lot. I was tall and very thin, my hair was jet-black and long, my skin was pale (even more than usual because of my eating disorder), I wore only clunky black boots or Doc Martens, which made my legs look even skinnier, and I spoke with alarming speed and said "fuck" a lot. I learned later that everyone at school thought I looked mean freshman year, but I wasn't mean at all. I was shy, and scared.

Lauren asked if I was a model because I looked like Kate Moss in the Calvin Klein ads that had become popular. It was a good thing to ask, because it made me feel pretty, and very skinny, but I smiled at her and shrugged off the suggestion.

As my parents and I were unpacking, Lauren's parents arrived in the room. Her dad reached out his hand to shake my dad's, introducing himself: "J.W., pleasure to meetcha." He pronounced the "W," "Dubya," and I giggled as my father started in response to JayDubya's vigorous, eager handshake, "Edward Said, yes, uh, very nice to meet you as well." The scenario seemed ridiculous somehow. My family always seemed normal to me until we were around new people. Then we always seemed foreign, unfamiliar with American mores.

After my parents said good-bye and hugged and kissed me so much that Wadie had to tell them to leave because we were "all being ridiculous," I went back up to the room to try to start my new life. People kept knocking on the door. First it was Lindsey, a girl I knew from summer camp, telling me where she and all the other people she was friends with already (if you'd gone to boarding school as she had, you showed up at college with an instant social group, it seemed) were going to be hanging out. I said I'd see about joining them later, and thanked her, but I didn't go. I was too shy. I didn't want to become friends with 345 people at once. I missed my friends from home.

There was a second knock on the door. My residential adviser appeared. "Oh my God," he said. "Hey! I didn't know that Edward Said was your dad! I mean, I can't *believe* I just met him!!! His book? *Orientalism?* I am probably gonna be quoting it, like, nine million times in my thesis!!! I mean, like, he is the very reason that Asian Americans such as, like, me, call ourselves *Asian Americans.* I mean, he is *why* no one says 'Oriental' anymore! Whoa. Wow. What an honor. *So* cool."

Lauren looked at me with curiosity. I smiled, and shrugged. My RA kept explaining to her about my dad. She nodded and listened eagerly. I sat on my bed and took the scene in. I was proud, of course, but I wasn't sure what I was supposed to do as "Edward Said's daughter." I had nothing to add to his philosophies or anything. So I just smiled.

The next day, everyone in the freshman class was required to attend a special lecture, just for us, given by Professor Cornel West. They'd sent us some reading ("Democratic Vistas," by Walt Whitman) to do over the summer, because that was what Prof West was going to be discussing.

I entered Alexander Hall with my RA group; we'd walked over together after dinner. The rest of the class of 1996 was trickling in from all sides of the auditorium. The stage was in the center of the room, and the seats went all the way around, like a stadium, or a theater set up in the round. I followed my new neighbors toward some seats at the opposite end of the room. As I brushed past the stage, Professor West, or "Brother Cornel," as I had been instructed to call him when I was twelve, caught sight of me. A huge grin took over his face. I smiled too, happy to feel recognized and known in the massive sea of newness that surrounded me on all sides. He pulled me up onto the stage. We embraced, and talked for a few minutes. Was I okay? he asked. Did I need anything? I could always call him, he reminded me; he would be looking out for me. I smiled, in order to hide the tears filling my eyes. He saw them anyway. He gave me another hug.

I jumped down off the stage to find my seat. As I climbed the risers, my new classmates began to shout out to me, "How do you know him?" "That's so cool!" "Wow. You know him?"

For a moment, I was very proud, and then, in an instant, I was mortified.

I knew who Cornel West was because I had met him in

my apartment when I was in seventh grade. He was a student of my dad's, and had come over to see him, but my dad had forgotten about the appointment. I let Cornel into the living room and then returned to my record player. My dad's secretary finally called me and told me that Daddy was across town and had completely forgotten the meeting. I walked back down our long hallway to the living room to convey Daddy's sincerest apologies, as I had been instructed. Cornel was facing away from me, looking at the books on the shelves. His arms behind his back, his glasses on the end of his nose, his pale blue three-piece suit picking up the light from the window that fell over the Hudson River, he looked to me like he had walked out of a TV show from the '70s. He turned around to face me as soon as he heard my footsteps. I delivered the message and relayed my father's intention to reschedule expediently. Cornel thanked me as I showed him out. Before I closed the door behind him, he leaned down to me and said, "Please give my love to Brother Edward and Sister Mariam, of course, and please let me tell you one thing, sweetheart. You are so kind, and so gracious, and lovely, but you should know this: You should *never* let a strange black man into your house when you're all alone. Promise me you won't ever do that again."

Bewildered, I nodded. He left.

Revered Princeton professor Cornel West was, to me, one of my dad's nine billion students, a family friend who sometimes came over for drinks. To many of my new classmates, he was reason enough to want to be at Princeton. I was embarrassed that I knew him better than everyone, but knew nothing of his work. For the next four years of my life, I had that feeling just about every day about many people I had grown up around. It was bizarre to the point of absurdity to imagine some nerdy, socially awkward old guy I'd shown to the bathroom of our apartment writing the books and essays I was assigned in class. But it was much more surreal when I began to realize how frequently the works of my own father were assigned, and in how many different fields of study. To put it bluntly, I very often felt like an idiot who, though she'd spent every day of her life around him, knew nothing of her father's achievements in the world of scholarship.

Apparently, they were monumental.

I majored in comparative literature, and received a certificate in theater and dance. Princeton was the perfect place for me to go to school, because all I wanted to do was read books in other languages, drink coffee, write in my journal, and listen to my music. Since most of my classes were in East Pyne Hall, where the Classics and Romance Languages and Literature departments were, I spent a lot of my time in the student center in that same building. Thus I was able to skip meals in the cafeteria (luckily my dorm was off campus) and eat alone (sometimes adhering to my doctor's meal plan, sometimes just sticking with Rice Krispies and frozen yogurt), and I was able to observe the social world of Princeton, participate when I liked, stay connected, and then retreat into a corner and hide when I needed to.

Because of my choice of major, the way that I dressed (short black skirts, black tights, merino wool or cashmere sweaters, with a scarf around my neck so I wouldn't freeze), the courses I took (The French Novel, French Drama, French Thought, French Poetry, Latin Poetry, Latin Drama, Dante, Virgil, Theater, Theater, Theater, and Theater), and the building in which I spent my time drinking black coffee, I unintentionally honed a new identity for my college self. No longer a WASP turned Jewish girl, I was now, truly, a "European Intellectual." I was equal parts punk miserable girl as well, which gave my persona a nice, unexpected, modern twist.

Ussama, my cousin who was in grad school, was often "forced" to introduce me to his friends and colleagues. "Naj," he'd say, "can I introduce you to so-and-so? He's a grad-student friend of mine, and he is madly in love with you."

I'd look at Ussama pleadingly. "Why is he in love with me? Has he met me? Or does he just see me around and think it would be superb to have an affair with Edward Said's daughter?" I had caught on to my father's intellectual rock-star status by this point, and was entirely aware that I myself was not the draw.

"Come on, Naj, of course you're stunning, charming, brilliant, and anyone would be honored to be in your presence . . . but also, yes, he's a big fan of Edward's. Please?"

Part of me still wanted to be a regular American coed, and the idea that all sorts of "professional nerds" (grad students) wanted to date me because they liked my dad's books made me shudder and want to run and hide under my bed. I was horrified by the thought of actually having to date one of these *actual* smart people, who would no doubt quickly discover that this particular apple had fallen far, far from the tree. That said, I certainly didn't mind if people thought I drank absinthe and read Proust on Saturday afternoons, even if I was more likely to be drinking an Ensure Plus and writing a food diary while listening to Pearl Jam. The truth was I did *not* want to go to Paris on the weekend and have a forty-five-year-old boyfriend who wrote poetry and smoked clove cigarettes. I still wanted to date the cute boys who wore baseball caps and called me "Dude."

BY ALL OBJECTIVE ACCOUNTS, I was in disastrous physical health during those years, and yet I managed to enjoy college immensely. I was sociable, relatively funny, and extremely self-deprecating in what I guess was a charming way, so I managed to have a pretty normal undergraduate life that consisted of beer (which, truth be told, I never drank because of the calories), pot (no calories), and general idiocy. When some people assumed my avoidance of beer meant I was Muslim, I started wearing a cross sometimes and carrying beer around and spilling it out on the floor to dispel any rumor that I was some "stereotypical Arab." I didn't have a serious boyfriend in the whole time I was at Princeton, but I didn't want one. I knew that guys were briefly fascinated by me because I looked different and dressed differently from most of the other girls, I had a sort of sad, soulful look in my big brown eyes, and I was the daughter of some larger-than-life intellectual. I was "exotic" and "enigmatic" and, therefore, by extension, "a creative genius with a deep sorrow inside" or something like that. Obviously, a lot of these perceptions were based on my sallow skin, dark hair, and mostly black clothing, and I most certainly played them up knowingly. I knew what *Orientalism* was about, and I was perfectly happy to let a nice all-American boy see what I was like for a minute or two, and then go back to his girlfriend. It was the perfect way to make sure no one got too close to me, truth be told. I had work to do, a meal plan to stick to, and a fragile ego to keep hold of; I didn't want a boyfriend.

Intellectually, though, I finally came into my own at Princeton. I found my own literary interests and favorite authors, and even when everyone else saw links to my father's work in my choice of thesis subject ("Ah, you love Genet because he loved the Palestinians and knew your father! Of course!"), I knew that these were my interests, not his.

It was relatively easy to avoid my Arab-ness in college too. In part it was because the Oslo Accords were signed in 1993, so to anyone who wasn't actually from Palestine or Israel, the Israelis and Palestinians seemed to be getting along fine; the war in Lebanon had ended and the country was being rebuilt, and I went to a school where political activity on campus was nonexistent.

I did join the Arab Society of Princeton, reluctantly, and at the urging of Wadie and Ussama, who actually hated it more than I did. Going to the weekly meeting was really just an excuse for the three of us to see one another. Since most of the Arab students at Princeton were princes who didn't need to worry about much, there were very few people at the gatherings anyway. Everyone who did show up would participate in a passionate two-hour argument about what our club's T-shirts should look like, and then the meeting would end. It was just like every other Arab assembly I'd ever seen in my life, actually. To Wadie and Ussama, the meetings were "useless" because they were "not political enough . . . but what do you expect at *Princeton*," they'd say.

Later, over coffee, they'd reenact the meeting, mocking each member and his personal, unwavering, and deeply felt opinion on the potential T-shirt design. I would giggle. I didn't care at all about the club. I just liked being around my family and hearing Arabic spoken.

By the time I was a senior, though, somehow I had inherited the job of president. I performed happily, and pretty passively. I quickly named an eager new member my vice president and dispatched him to organize a fund-raising party. I made only one demand: there had to be lots of hummus and tabouli to eat at the party (if you feed people, they'll support you). Once the money was raised, I left it to the underclassmen to find someone to bring in for a lecture, and moved on.

Unlike Wadie, I still didn't really care about politics and history, and I couldn't fully express myself in the language. And yet, when I found the friend at Princeton who made me feel the safest, the happiest, and the least weird, it did not escape me that her father was originally from the Middle East.

Leonora was born in London and raised in Manhattan, and then Maine. She went to Brearley, and to boarding school in Massachusetts. Her mother had been raised in New York City and was a Chapin girl herself. Her father, like mine, went to Princeton. And her father had also been born in the Middle East, his parents originally from Iraq.

His older brother had actually gone to elementary school with my dad in Cairo. And Teta Wadad, in her memoir, had written about members of Leonora's family who came to Lebanon during the summer and often visited with my great-grandfather. Though Leonora's dad's family was Jewish, they were a part of the Middle East as my parents had known it, and in that regard, our families had more in common than not. And so even though we arrived at the WASP, Jewish, Middle Eastern, private school, European place in entirely different ways, and precisely because Leonora was *actually* all of those things in one human body, and *was* pretty and smart and fun and normal and funny, I felt much less alone.

FURIOUSLY WRITING my senior thesis—about the "metatheatricality of theater"—I realized both that I was good at this academic writing and that something felt off. I understood so deeply what I was writing about, but it did not seem right that I should spend my life writing about it for other academics. Initially, I had thought I would just keep going to school, get a Ph.D. like everyone else in my family, and settle into the comfort and safety of academic life. But as I typed, my fingers itched and I bounced up and down in my seat. I kept going back to a notebook on which

I had written the quote "Writing about art is like dancing about architecture" in huge letters with a Sharpie. The acting classes I had begun attending at age eight to help ease me out of my shyness had worked. I had performed in countless plays and showcases and taken many more classes since I was in the third grade, and I knew I was a good actress.

I announced to the world that I was taking a year to pursue acting and see what happened.

My parents indulged me in this idea and I set out to achieve success in this new field in the same manner I had done everything else and succeeded. I would go to the best school, work hard at being good and pretty and doing things "right," and I would be ultimately validated and celebrated and noticed.

So I set out to become a professional actress, not knowing that other people could tell that who I tried to be on the outside—a skinny, talented, smart, '90s version of Audrey Hepburn's character in *Funny Face*—was not at all who I was on the inside. My career plans conflicted with my arduous anorexia treatment (now in its fifth year—I would gain till I was "okay" and then go lose it all again). I was a professional actress struggling to overcome an eating disorder *before* she actually made it in the business.

I discovered in a summer Shakespeare program at the Public Theater in New York City and in the conservatory classes that followed that "taking up space" was something that I had to learn to do, in more ways than one. I was told I was not really a full human being but needed to become one in order to be able to succeed in my chosen field. I not only needed to literally gain weight, I needed to figure out who I was.

This process would become further complicated as I ventured into the commercial world with the name Najla Said. I was repeatedly and constantly described by casting directors and agents as "ethnic" and then just as often rejected with, "No! You're like a Jewish Italian girl from New York. You're too white to be ethnic." I struggled to figure out which I was. I refused to change my name. I had no deep attachment to my culture, but I felt very strongly that I should not have to do something so arcane to be seen for all that I was. I felt that deep painful racist punch in my stomach every time I even considered the idea of becoming "Nancy Smith" so that I could get a job. I pressed on. My friends began to succeed.

But I kept going. I did everything I was supposed to do; I auditioned for a million plays and programs and got rejected, I did some shows in theaters on whose front doors homeless people sometimes left their own excrement as a calling card, in theaters with cats running around inside them. I auditioned for the prestigious MFA acting programs at NYU, Juilliard, and Yale, and was rejected. The head of one of them, whom I knew already from a class I'd taken elsewhere, told me, "You don't need to go to school. You are good at school, Najla. I think you need to live—get your heart broken, struggle to pay rent, travel, *have fun, even!*"

"No, but I do have to go to grad school, 'cause that's really the only way to get an agent, and also my parents won't take me seriously until I have a master's in something, and actually, *I* won't take me seriously until I have outside proof that I'm allowed to be an actress!"

Needless to say, I didn't go anywhere. But I kept on. After a few years of hostessing in restaurants and teaching acting to kids for very little money, I got a job tutoring eighth-graders for the tests to get into private high school, and high school students for the SATs.

I didn't want to like my job or be good at it, but I was. And I loved the students too. They were adorable and wonderful and reminded me of myself in high school. I could never press upon them how much it didn't matter what they got on their tests, or how much their lives would not be ruined if they didn't get into Harvard. It was refreshing to take note of how much I'd actually grown up in that regard.

❧

SEVEN OUT OF TEN TIMES the student I tutored went to a Jewish day school, and sometimes, according to my boss, I was not supposed to call the house on a Saturday.

None of that fazed me, but I was always a bit surprised to realize that even sometimes when I said I was Arab, the parents of these kids still couldn't always believe I wasn't Jewish. I was "so Upper West Side," "so self-deprecating and funny," I knew what all the Jewish holidays were about, and I certainly didn't seem even slightly uncomfortable in a Jewish home. One of the first experiences I had in this regard was very early on. I was tutoring an eighth-grade boy who went to a Jewish school on the Upper West Side. Just before Thanksgiving, as I was leaving his apartment, I told his mom that I wouldn't be there the following week-end because I was going to San Francisco for my brother's wedding.

"Oh, how nice! Where are they getting married?" she asked.

"In a big mansion thingie, I think? I am not totally sure . . . They have these houses that are really wedding spaces in Pacific Heights. It's apparently quite beautiful."

"Oh, and will it be a traditional service?"

"Um, I'm not sure. I mean, I don't know what they decided, but I am sure they'll have some Arabic music and stuff."

"No, but I mean, *the service*, will it be a traditional Se-phardic service?"

At this point in the conversation, her thirteen-year-old son jumped in. "Mom! She's Lebanese."

"Yeah, we are Leb . . ." My voice trailed off. I decided not to continue talking lest I disappoint her. She *really* wanted me to be Jewish. "Anyway, so, I'll see you the following week, and we can schedule an extra session for a makeup. Happy Thanksgiving!" I gave her my biggest, cheesiest good-girl smile and left the apartment, half amused, half terrified she'd find out I wasn't Jewish and then begin to hate me. I was glad to have the two-week break before I saw her again.

MEANWHILE, I STARTED returning to Lebanon more often, and I began to reconnect with my culture and my place in it. As the country flourished and reemerged from the ashes of the fifteen-year civil war, I found myself flourishing too. It took some years, of course, but I slowly began to be able to nourish myself, not only with the food my relatives fed me but with the love that they gave me, and the opportunity to be part of a culture that embraced me fully.

For the most part, my trips to Lebanon kept me in the ever-changing, happily rebooming capital of Beirut, with its nightclubs, beach parties, incredible shopping, and relative freedom. The city is, and has always been, mixed and international. The Lebanese have always had a particular love of fashion, style, and "the latest thing"—the war has not destroyed this. Women wear Chanel, get their hair and nails done religiously, agonize over the right shoes, and tan themselves idly in expensive bikinis while wearing enormous designer sunglasses and eating carrots. The men are similar; they display a love of fashion, cologne, and automobiles that is unparalleled, and their own grooming habits are no less involved. It's kind of like L.A. But it's not. It's between Israel and Syria, it's divided along sectarian lines, and it is a constantly ticking time bomb of political instability. There are also Palestinian refugee camps all over the place. But you don't see those unless you try, or unless you live in one.

I wish I could articulately explain to the world—and to my younger self!—how the Middle East really works. I wish I could help everyone discover all the wonderful things that I was lucky enough to be able to rediscover about it, all of the little details that make the culture so incredibly addictive and captivating. Ironically, every time I try, I end up sounding like a rabid Orientalist. Nonetheless, here is what I have come to love about this world.

There is indeed the muezzin, the call to prayer, amazing at twilight, and there is that mysterious, deeply spiritual feel of the air and water (you are almost constantly aware that all the Bible stuff happened *here*). There are the smells and sounds and spices and flavors and carpets and hookahs, I suppose, if you're looking at it that way, but what really grabs you about this very electric, vibrant culture is that everyone who is talking to *you* is talking to *you* and looking at *you* and thinking about *you* and trying to make *you* (another person) feel good and comfortable and good and content. The Arabic language is a perfect example of how this works. Let's say that you have ordered something at a restaurant or you have just gotten out of a taxi and you would like to say "thank you" to the waiter or the driver. You actually would not say "thank you," though we do have a word for it. You would most probably say "God bless your hands"—*"Yislam eedayk"*—or "God give you strength"—*"Allah y'ateek il afieh"*—or another equally lovely phrase. "God bless your hands"—just take a moment to think about what a nice thing that is to say to someone. Do bear in mind that you would say those words to *anyone*—a Christian, a Muslim, a Jew, a Buddhist, or an atheist. The word *Allah* in Arabic means "God." It does *not* mean some other special, fundamentalist Islamic deity who hates infidels. It is a word whose denotation is "the supreme being." Thus, in the same way that Spanish-speaking people call him *Dios* and the French call him *Dieu, Allah* is just God. In English, we often say things like "God rest his soul" and "Oh my God," but somehow I feel like we're taught here in America that if an Arab says something similar, he is a fundamentalist Muslim urging all believers to destroy the infidels. That's just not even a little bit true.

I love the way that everyone calls you by a nickname, always. They just constantly multiply, the nicknames. They're often diminutives of your actual name. (Mona becomes "Mon-Moon," Sana "Sansoon," Tala "Taltool." My name—Najla—becomes "Najjoolie," "Najjoultie," "Najnoojie," "Noonie," and, of course, "Naji".) If not by a nickname, you will most certainly be called by a pet name at least five times an hour. I find them so delightful: *habibi*, or its feminine, *habibti*, is the most well known. It literally means "the one I love." There is also *hayati* ("my life"), *eyooni* ("my eyes"), *rouhee* ("my soul"), *albi* ("my heart"), and *amoora* ("like the moon"). I think that, in a way, it is from the language and the way people use it that life becomes this lovely thing. You share it with other people, you delight in their delight, you want to feed them, love them, laugh with them, make them feel good. It's nice.

Also, people just stop by to visit you. And it's not weird, it's lovely! On cell phones, no one has voice mail. If you get a "missed call," you call the number back. It is as if the whole idea is to *connect* with other people—not avoid them. I think, from all of that, comes a need to go out and touch and love and dance and eat. It's as if you are on a constant quest to meet everyone.

I certainly don't know all twenty-two Arab countries. My personal knowledge is only of Lebanon and Palestine. But it seems to me that all of the things that people love about Greece and Italy—you know, the way people drive wherever they want whenever they want in whatever direction they want, the way people get insanely angry for a moment and then five minutes later are kissing you, all of those "Mediterranean" things—they're true of *all* of the Mediterranean peoples, Mediterranean Arabs included.

We are really not that different from the rest of the world—Arabs.

ℰℐ

IN THE SUMMER OF 2000, just after my dad had undergone another round of chemotherapy, we were in Beirut for my cousin Karim's wedding, and my best friend (or "gay boyfriend," as I prefer to call him), Francesco, came along as my date. Since he is Sicilian by way of Brooklyn, he had very quickly become close with my immediate family. What he heard about Lebanon reminded him a lot of where he comes from in the Mediterranean. He met my cousins, aunts, uncles, and friends (who all wondered if I knew that my "boyfriend" was a homosexual but never asked, because, apparently, that would be rude), and they all fell in love with him.

We spent most of our time at the beach, but one day Francesco, Wadie, his fiancée, Jennifer, Mommy, Daddy, and I traveled to the south to visit the border between Palestine and Lebanon. The Israelis had just relinquished their occupation of that area, and a tour of the area had been arranged for my father.

On the drive down the coast, the fancy beach clubs gave way to makeshift seaside camps—where portions of the population settled after losing their homes during the war. The temperature rose. It got hotter, hotter, and hotter as we drove. Billboards advertising suntan oil and fast-food restaurants were gradually replaced by posters of bearded, turban-wearing men. I shuddered. My comfort in the Middle East was still very new, and I realize now that at that time it was a comfort that I had felt only in and around the urban, cosmopolitan areas of Beirut. My heart pounded loudly in my chest. I was suddenly scared, and I felt the same constricted "I don't belong here" feeling I had felt when I had gone to Palestine, eight years earlier.

We got to the actual Lebanon-Israel border. My brother and I stood there and posed for pictures at the "crossroads of our identity" . . . or whatever you want to call it. Just across the wire was Israel. Palestine—I hadn't been there since 1992. There it was. So close but, oh yes, so far away. A truck drove up the mountain straight in front of us. It was close enough that we could read the Hebrew writing. I felt my heart jump into my throat and my insides turn.

Before we headed back to Beirut, one of our friends and tour guides insisted we visit one more important place, an abandoned Israeli checkpoint tower, which had become a place of pilgrimage for visitors to the area. In a gesture of solidarity with those who until a month before had lived under military occupation, people now came here and one by one threw rocks toward the abandoned tower, in a symbolic gesture of joy at the liberation of the land. The tower was on the Lebanese side, and the Israelis had left the country, so there was nothing on either side for miles and miles except a bunch of scraggly rocks here and there.

My brother said, "Look how badly they throw around here; their rocks land nowhere near the tower—it's 'cause they don't play baseball." Then he picked up a rock and threw it, pretty far, into the empty, dry land. My father, never one to be outdone, suddenly wanted to show that he could throw just as far as, if not farther than, my brother. I cowered in a corner, waiting for some ridiculously disproportionate military response to their stupidity, which thankfully did not come. What did come, however, was even more ridiculous. One of the photographers we were with decided this would make a great shot—*Edward Said throwing a rock in solidarity with the people of Southern Lebanon.* And so, by the time we got back to Beirut two hours later, the photo was all over the Internet, and there was outrage at home, as the *New York Post* had featured the picture with a story about my dad's "terrorist activities" and people were coming out of the woodwork to demand he be fired from Columbia.

Wait—what?

Apparently, although a revered professor at Columbia, Edward Said was also a terrorist who had viciously attacked an Israeli soldier in southern Lebanon.

Francesco's reaction to the incident reminded me I wasn't crazy. I had grown used to these kinds of press distortions and was sick of being called a conspiracy theorist by my American friends every time I pointed them out, so I had learned to keep them to myself. But Francesco was outraged, and he wasn't Arab or even remotely interested in politics.

"I don't understand what is going on. These people are crazy. That's not what happened at all. I have pictures, I can show anyone who asks that that's not what happened. I am so confused by America right now."

I looked at him, relieved. I needed to hear his reaction to make sure mine was legitimate.

When my dad heard that Francesco had photos showing the abandoned checkpoint tower and the vast area of nothing around it, he called him immediately.

"I *must* have them. These people are after me! I *must* clear my name!"

I look back on this event as the beginning of the end of

my father's spirit. Between the backlash at Columbia, the Second Intifada beginning in Palestine that fall, and the crowning event, 9/11, Daddy stopped speaking to the American media. He wrote for the Arab press more, and agreed to do interviews only for the BBC or other European media outlets that would give him more than a two-minute sound bite to explain "why they hate us."

On the morning the towers fell, I had gone to the gym. I walked in and saw everyone staring at TV screens. I listened a moment to the speculation about a misguided plane that had maybe lost control and hit the tower. I proceeded up by elevator to the workout floor. The door opened and I was nearly knocked over by CBS correspondent Ed Bradley, who was rushing to work. Then the second plane hit. For the next hour I sat on the floor with trainers and other members of the gym, although some poor exercise-addicted souls couldn't stop working out even as the horrific morning unfolded. One guy was walking around the weight area with a radio plugged into his ears, giving us the latest updates as if he were a train conductor:

"They got the Pentagon!" he bellowed across the gym.

"Plane down in Pennsylvania," he continued, and I slowly got hotter and hotter and hotter inside. I felt as if I could pinpoint the exact *moment* when everyone in the immediate vicinity came to the collective, silent conclusion that this nightmare was most certainly being carried out by "Arab terrorists." I think I can safely say, as clichéd as it sounds, that *that* was the moment my life changed forever.

Without comparing my reaction to that day to anyone else's or making it sound more significant, I want to explain what happened to me.

First of all, for those of us born and bred on the streets of New York City, this event was an unbelievable attack on *home*. Not home in the sense of *America*, but in the sense of *my house, my world, my life*. Many people talk of the overwhelming tingly joyous feeling that you get when you see the New York skyline out of an airplane window, or from across the bridge in New Jersey. Take that feeling, imagine it, and then add to it the feeling you get when you realize you are *home*—whatever that means to you. That's how it was a little different for us New Yorkers. After that day, a lot of people freaked out and drove back to Pennsylvania or Vermont or wherever their family was. I couldn't do that. Home was here, "under attack."

Back at the gym, I was now standing side by side with

one of the trainers, watching the events unfold. I knew him a little, and maybe I stood with him because of that; to feel close to someone in a room full of strangers.

With one eye still on the TV, he casually turned to me and said: "This is clearly the work of Palestinians—it's an act that has Arafat written all over it!!!"

That was it for me; for the first time in my life, and with a heat that surprised me, I lunged into him.

"*What are you talking about?* When has Arafat ever driven a plane into a building, attacked America physically? He's never done anything like this, and now he has his Nobel Peace Prize—this wouldn't be good PR, now, would it? And where in God's name would 'the Palestinians'— who have no money, no resources, no access to movement even out of their neighborhoods, no internal structure— *where* and *how* and *why* would they pull this off? Do you *not* understand that they don't want all of America to be destroyed? If they *could* do something like this why wouldn't they do it to Israel? It would seem a little more efficient! No? Do you even remember the Oklahoma City bombing? Everyone blamed us then too, but they were *wrong,* weren't they?"

My head was spinning a little. I immediately ran out of the gym. I called Daddy and got voice mail (as everyone did that day: almost any calls that were actually connected went to voice mail). "Daddy, what is this? Are you okay?

What's happening? Did we do this? *Why* would we do this?"

As soon as I said those words I had a panic attack. I said "we"! I said "we"!! "They" would come after me now for saying that, wouldn't they?

I just meant Arabs, that's all I meant. I wanted confirmation that I wasn't wrong about my conception of "Palestinians."

I wasn't. When you've seen both sides of the story, when you've been on the other side of media spin, it becomes easier to see the truth and to defend it. That's all I was doing. That's all I suppose Daddy had ever done. But it's so hard to stand by it when everyone around you is just not hearing you.

I tried to stay at my parents' apartment the next couple of nights. But it was difficult to sleep, in part because I thought "they" were coming to blow us up. By "they" I meant the "Islamic terrorists" who would have no prior knowledge of the nice Arabs in the building (nor would they have cared about us actually, according to the news reports—if we were Muslims, we would be martyrs in our death, and then, of course, since we were Christians we were infidels anyway). But by "they" I also meant "the Americans" who would most certainly be coming to root us out.

Place on top of these fears a little post-traumatic stress

from having been in Lebanon as a child during the war, as well as the thought that if Palestine, Lebanon, *and* New York aren't safe, then where on this earth do I go?

Thus I was crowned and outed as an "Arab-American." I'd never been a hyphenate before—at first it was kind of nice to be an officially franchised minority, but then it was horrifying. This part is sort of hard to explain. I don't feel entirely American, never have, but it's not because I don't want to or because I don't seem it—I do want to, I do seem it. I don't feel entirely Arab though either, for the same reasons. But I also certainly don't feel like any *combination of the two.*

People are always shocked to know that my father wasn't a fan of this identity-politics, PC movement of calling yourself a "a Pacific Islander from the third island to the right of Samoa hyphen American." I guess it makes sense that someone who championed the rights and humanity of the "other" would be a fan of declaring yourself an "African American," or whatever. But he wasn't. And that makes sense too. Daddy didn't like labels—"Oriental" was the one he was most famous for disliking, but it was just an example of millions of others.

He once explained:

"And so there are two alternatives: either you go in and just obliterate your past, which some people have tried to do, or you cultivate your identity with a group of yourself, like the Koreans do that. You know, whole parts of New Jersey which are completely Korean: they have their own stores and they live together and they speak Korean to each other. Arabs don't tend to do that. Well, there aren't that many of us. And they're more spread out. Maybe they do in Detroit . . . Mostly they, you know, assimilate. Become part of the melting pot. In Canada they have a mosaic theory. People retain their identity, and belong to all of Canada. America's an assimilationist model, where people become American, and America overrides everything else."

A month later, on a Tuesday evening, I rode the L train to Williamsburg, Brooklyn, to attend a meeting. I wasn't sure I totally wanted to go. There had been a listserve for years, ArabDrama it was called, for theater artists of Arab descent all over the world. We had gotten to know one another by our e-mail monikers, initials, and postings—some interesting, helpful, informative; some ridiculous, maddening. We had laughed together, fought with one another, helped one another, become friends in that bizarre new way that the Internet allowed us to. For most of us, newly crowned "Arab-Americans" by the agents and casting directors we had been getting to know, it was an opportunity to dip our foot in the waters of being Arab-American without diving all the way in. We had all been told, time and again:

"You have to find a niche."

"Rather than trying to stand out in a room of 6,453 brown-haired twenty-something women, stand out in a room of ten Arab-looking women, and book the show. Then you can do what you want!"

"Even Jennifer Lopez had to play Selena to get famous. Now she can play a Chinese man if she wants to, because she's *Jennifer Lopez!*"

"You can play *so* many things, but this one is really hot right now, so let's try to make use of that *skill* that you have that is unique to you!"

Early in the summer, one of the girls had messaged the group saying, "Who is in New York? Do you want to try to meet up in person?"

I read the e-mail. I read the responses. I knew who was going. I followed the planning. I kept silent. I wanted to go, eventually, but not now. I wanted to go, but not alone; I wasn't ready. Anyway, they met on Tuesdays, and I tutored kids every weekday night; I could never go on a Tuesday. I'll go when my schedule clears up, in early November, I decided.

I stuck to my plan, but found myself free a few weeks earlier. Since 9/11 had landed squarely in the middle of my warming-up-to-join-an-Arab-American-theater-company time, I knew I had to go.

Another girl, a Palestinian American playwright I knew, told me she was going that night. We met up after

I finished tutoring and took the subway together. I was glad I was not alone. She told me about the people who were usually at the meetings; some of the boys were cute, she said. I didn't care. I looked at her, fascinated. "You like Arab men?"

She nodded.

We got to the meeting on time, and I was introduced. The meeting was run by a short-haired beauty named Maha. She scared me, but I loved her. I loved her boots, her clothes, her bag; I could tell she grew up in London.

I quickly learned that this group, made up of mostly actors—Rana, Maha, Omar M, Omar K, Leila, James, and Afaf—had met just a few times and had started to work on a theater project about Arabs in America, but weren't in any real hurry to get it done. Now, for obvious reasons, it seemed urgent.

I mostly listened as they talked about trying to set a goal for the project, but piped up when they started talking about wanting to perform at the American-Arab Anti-Discrimination Committee (ADC) conference. I thought it was funny that they were strategizing how to approach the people in charge about performing at that boring nightmare I had been dragged to every year of my childhood.

"Um, I can help with that. I mean, that's not a problem. I can get you into the ADC conference."

My parents were founding members of the ADC. I never thought anything of it. I felt vaguely proud of them as I explained that I knew the president of the organization well and could just ask him.

The second goal was to get the show—a documentary-style theater project in which random people's interviews, initiated by the question "What comes to mind when you hear the word 'Arab'?" were edited together into a collage—into performance by the following summer, for the New York International Fringe Festival. Maha closed the meeting by going around the circle, taking stock of who wanted to do what in the project:

"So, Leila, you want to interview and act; Omar M, same; Afaf, same; James, same; Omar K, same; Rana, you'll help us out, like, as a consultant, and . . ."

She'd arrived at me.

"You. What are you, just here *watching*? Or . . . what?"

She kind of scared me.

"Well, I'll do whatever, but I'm an actress and I can do interviews if you like."

Her face softened. She smiled.

"Oh, cool! Nice! Okay. Najla—N-A-J-L-A? . . ." She started writing it down.

Most of us rode the L train back to Manhattan together. As we walked to the subway, Omar M introduced himself properly. "Hi, I'm Omar. It is nice to have you with us, Najla."

"Thanks." I smiled.

Omar M was *not* ugly.

Maha turned to me on the subway and asked, "So . . . 'Najla'—that's such a pretty name . . . I know it's Arabic, but I don't know it. What does it mean?"

"It means 'big black eyes like a cow,'" I told her with the "I am so proud of my special name, isn't it exotic and beautiful" smile I had now perfected.

"Wait, that's so weird! I'm pretty sure that's what my name means too!"

"Wait, what? No. 'Maha'? Are you sure? Maybe you have it confused with something else? I mean . . . well, not that you don't know what your own name means, but, I mean, that doesn't make sense, does it? That two names that don't even sound alike would have the same *random* meaning?"

"No, I swear, Maha means 'big black eyes like a cow' too."

"Oh my God, Arabic is so weird," I blurted out.

She laughed. "Yes, oh yes, it is."

I smiled.

Maha started imitating her Syrian father's accent.

I giggled and nodded my head. "Yes! Just like my mom!" I cried.

I liked these people.

As soon as I got home, I called my parents to tell them about my evening. I was excited and spoke a mile a minute. I needed them to give me this person's number and that person's e-mail so I could get us money and get us into the ADC convention. They said they'd give me the information the next day. They seemed so happy that I had finally interacted with some Arabs.

"Oh! Mommy! I forgot! So there was this girl at the meeting? Maha?"

"Maha who? Maybe I know her parents."

"Maha something I can't pronounce, *listen*!!! So, she just told me that her name means 'big black eyes like a cow' too. Is that true? Or—I mean, she is confused, right?"

"Eh . . . ehm . . . well . . ."

Her hesitation betrayed her guilt.

"Mommy!"

"Wait a minute, Naji," she finally said. "They are similar. But they are different."

"How are they different? I mean, I don't see how there is a lot of room for variety in 'big black eyes like a cow'!"

"Wait. Please. Give me a minute. I have to think about it."

I hung up the phone, and I left her to "think about it."

Meanwhile, I went to my computer and found a website of Arabic baby names. I looked up "Najla" and I looked up "Maha," and sure enough, I found them to mean essentially the same thing. But what is *weirder* is that not only was there a name that means "one with full rounded breasts," but there were also about twenty other names that mean "big black eyes like a . . . something"—"big black eyes like a cow," "big black eyes like a donkey," "big black eyes like a horse," "big black eyes like a monkey" . . .

Feeling betrayed, I sought out my greatest ally, Wadie.

"Oh yeah, Naj, they're similar, but they're not exactly the same, that website is wrong, of course. 'Maha' actually means 'big black eyes like an ibex' . . . or rather, an oryx, I believe? I have to check which."

Um, okay.

". . . but yeah, so it's not totally the same. And plus, 'Najla' has a second meaning anyway. It came up in my Arabic class once, in college."

"Really? What?"

"'Najla' also means . . . hold on, I'm checking the dictionary . . . Okay . . . okay . . . Here it is . . . Okay, 'Najla' also means . . . 'gaping wound.'"

Um.

Now, meanwhile, I have learned that my last name, contrary to what you might think, does not mean "big talker." "Said" actually means "happy" in Arabic, or as my father told me: "Not 'happy' as in 'la-la'" (he said this with a big goofy smile, and a rhythmic tilting of his head from side to side meant to indicate the idiocy of such happiness). "But, rather, a more *profound* sense of contentment." As he pronounced each syllable of the word "profound," he placed an open palm in front of his face and slowly lowered it toward his navel, indicating depth.

And my middle name, which was my maternal grandmother's name, "Wadad," means "love."

Put all that together and I, Najla Wadad Said, am literally, "a happy gaping wound of love."

Funny thing is, the more I think about it, the more I realize that it kind of fits. Perfectly.

❧

As the year wore on, our little theater group became my family. Afaf and Leila and Maha were my long-lost sisters—Arab somehow, but American really, and kind of European too. Maha and Afaf had been raised in London but had gone to American schools, and Leila was Lebanese on her mom's side and American on her dad's and had spent her childhood partly in Iraq, partly in D.C. James, Omar M, and Omar K were my sweet, loving brothers. We often used our meetings to bond about feeling weird in the months following 9/11. Most of us had just been trying to have a career for the past few years; we were just getting used to saying "I am an actor." And now, suddenly, we were both being told to add and feeling the need to add the words "Arab-American" to our job title.

It felt wrong to resist the label, given the fact that we didn't have anything against our families or our culture, but it also felt wrong to embrace it, because none of us knew what exactly an Arab-American was.

And when we did our interviews, we found that most of the people who *were* Arab used words like "love," "food," "home," "family," "laughter" when we asked them what the word "Arab" evoked. And most of the people who were not Arab used words like "sand," "desert," "camel," "terror," "mad," "angry," "Muslim."

It compelled us to keep going.

I got to know both my parents in a new way that year. I interviewed my mom for the show, and she became everyone's favorite character. She told me that in 1967, she'd seen Israeli flags flying up and down Fifth Avenue, "celebrating Israel's victory, which they called 'our victory'" in the Arab-Israeli war of that year, which made her feel so alone, and so strange. I wanted to know more.

James and Omar M interviewed Daddy, and his presence as a character in the play excited many people, including me, but it was not a new thing to hear him speak about Arabs in America. It was Mommy's interview that interested me more. She spoke so well of her culture and language. She told me how she came here as an exchange student in the early '60s, and was asked to pose for a local Pennsylvania paper in her "native garb." She wore the bizarre ancient costume for the photo but didn't understand why she had to do so; no one in Lebanon dressed like that, ever. She laughed as she recalled how people had asked her if she went to school on a camel. And even though by 2001 she had lived here for so many years, she retained so much pride in her Arab-ness. One of her stories became our favorite speech in the play, her lilting accent reminded all of us of our many cherished relatives. It also put into words one of the most common, seemingly simple, but really quite enormous differences between Arab culture and Western culture:

> When I first came to—to this country, ah, the first time I came, in '63, there was no—nobody knew what yogurt is. Well, you see, yogurt, in the Arab World is part of our everyday . . . food, and part of our life. We drink it and we call it eye-ran, and we . . . add it to the rice, and we add it to this dish or that dis—dish, and we, we drip it and we eat it as—for breakfast as labne every day so for me, yogurt ha—is assoshi-ay-ted with being sour and this wonderful, white milk, eh—that is sour in taste. When I came back in '67, it was at the beginning of the craze of yogurt in this country and yogurt was, um, flavored. Flavored with rahzburys and strawburys and blueburys, a—and I could not eat that stuff. And I found it very strange.

When the show finally went up, in August of 2002, we were exhausted. Proud, elated, excited, overwhelmed, and exhausted. We were ready to take over the world with our company, we felt like we'd found our own voices, our way into our culture, but we also needed to rest and process everything we'd done. I was especially excited at how proud my parents seemed to be of me, finally. And I had become captivated by the stories of their lives. I was exceedingly proud of them, for coming here to the States alone as really young people, for confronting racism head-on, for not giving in and hiding their Arab identity, in the way I had always wanted to do. For never, ever giving in to petty sectarian and nationalistic nonsense, and for always being humanists, no matter how many times they were still called terrorists. I was proud of them for raising me and Wadie in America and never making us feel like we were less than anyone, and for never giving up on us. I had fallen in love with my family and everything they stood for, even as, for the first time, I was feeling hatred and racism directed at me from fellow Americans.

My mother said to me: "Ever since you made Arab friends, you have really calmed down."

I laughed, remembering a similar thing she'd said to me in college about my friendship with Leonora.

"Well, I had to find my own friends, Mommy. I had to find people who were like me. I can't be friends with people just because they're Arab, and I never could. I wasn't resisting the embrace of it all because I *wanted to*, but because I felt completely alone. Now I guess I don't."

She grinned.

☙

DADDY HAD BEEN in the hospital that summer, with pneumonia. He'd gotten very gaunt, and had grown a beard because the doctors had told him not to shave. If he cut himself, it could be very dangerous, we were told, given the treatment he was receiving. It was the eleventh summer of Daddy's illness. Most of his rigorous and often dangerous treatments took place in the summer, so that he could teach during the school year, and every summer we assumed our roles as his caretakers.

The summer of 2003 Daddy got sick again, but this time was different.

On the night of August 14, 2003, a huge blackout struck New York and much of the eastern United States. I walked forty blocks in the sweltering heat and then up twelve flights of stairs to spend the night with my family, since my apartment was too small and ill-equipped for me to do nothing, alone, in the dark for an entire day. I was exhausted at the time, but I now think of that night as a gift. My parents were supposed to go to Europe that evening, for a month, but their flight had been canceled. Daddy's doctor was actually relieved that he would have to postpone his travel plans a few days; his immune system was already pretty compromised; airplanes and foreign air would only make it worse.

Daddy was in typical Daddy form that evening. As Mommy, Wadie, his wife, Jennifer, and I went up and down the stairs numerous times in order to stock up on water and other provisions, Daddy lay on the couch in the family room, gossiping away on the phone. He was talking to someone in Europe, declaring in a loud voice, "No—it's *unbelievable*," and then adding—a bit melodramatically, of course—"it's outrageous; we have to go *forage for food*!" as he glanced over at the three of *us* lugging packages into the apartment. Francesco called from L.A.—"Why am I not surprised that there is no power in the entire eastern half of the United States but for some reason Edward Said's phone is still working?"

After a simple dinner of lettuce, tuna fish, bread, and everything else perishable in the kitchen, we all sat in the living room and talked by candlelight; there was nothing else to do. Mommy had a sly smile on her fatigued face; she was secretly overjoyed that we were all together. Daddy, uncharacteristically in a pair of shorts (it was *that* hot), declared that we had to have a serious discussion. He joked that he could not survive without air-conditioning and that the four of us would have to work in *punkah-wallah* shifts (yes, he used that word), fanning him during the night. He then launched into the telling of a "famous" Tolstoy story as we sat and listened. In the same way he had done when we were little, Daddy added details and changed character names to make the story more interesting. As usual, nobody said anything, except me.

"That's not a Tolstoy story, Daddy!"

"Naj, be quiet. You don't know this one, it's rare, now shhhh! Let me finish! It's good!" he retorted, but the smirk on his face betrayed him. We all looked at one another and burst out laughing. He was sometimes such a little boy.

Eventually it grew so dark that we all retired to our rooms. I woke early the next morning, desperate to have my e-mail back, in case my very recently ex-boyfriend had been trying to reach me (yes, I am aware that he, also a New Yorker, had no more electricity than I did). When the power came back on in the morning, I packed up my bag and made my way to the front door, until Daddy stopped me.

"Naj, where are you *going*?"

"Home. It's over. There's electricity. I have to do stuff."

"Don't be silly. Stay. There is electricity in *some* places, but it's going to be a long time before anything is back to normal. Don't you like it here?"

I laughed. "I do, Daddy. I love it here. But I want to go home now."

"How about some juice?"

"Daddy, I tell you every time you ask me that that I can't drink juice! It burns my esophagus."

"Oh, my little Naj, she's a true artist in every sense! Even the orange juice hurts. I love it!"

"'Bye, Daddy. Have a good time in Spain."

"'Bye, little Naj. I love you. Don't forget to call me."

My parents went to Europe the next day. While they were away, Daddy got sick. Every night in the middle of the night, he'd wake delirious, with a very high fever. They came back early, and he was admitted to the hospital. They couldn't find an infection, but he stayed there for a week or two, undergoing test after test after test. Whatever he had, it wasn't viral, and it didn't seem to be bacterial either. I registered the oddity of it, but I assumed he'd be okay and so did everyone else. He always got sick in the summer, and then he always got better.

He asked to go home. His room in the hospital was meant to be germ free; anyone who entered had to wear a mask, and there was antibacterial lotion everywhere. You weren't allowed to even enter the room without putting it on your hands. But the whole process seemed a charade. The hospital was filthier than home, and Daddy knew it. He also knew, I think, that he was dying, and he wanted to go home first.

The next few days, Daddy acted very strange. He said

it was because of the medicine they gave him, and it was, partially, but it was also because he was trying to say good-bye. He cried often (a symptom of the medicine) and was extremely loving to everyone around him. Most poignantly, he cried when he introduced my aunt Grace, who had arrived in New York that week out of concern for his health, to a friend. "Do you know my little sister?" he'd said, and had begun to weep. Wadie and I had giggled nervously. I'd seen Daddy cry twice in my life: once at Teta Hilda's funeral, and once when I went with him for a bone-marrow biopsy. The needle was longer and bigger than any I had ever seen, and Daddy squeezed my hand and sobbed when they poked his sacrum with it. The needle made the most horrific and comically loud *pop!* when it penetrated the bone. I felt my heart crack both times I saw tears in Daddy's eyes, but now all I could do was giggle. I felt awful.

He began to have crazy dreams, some prophetic, some just heartbreakingly profound. One night he woke up certain his watch was cracked. Another night he woke and began haphazardly throwing items into a suitcase. He told my mother, in Arabic, that they had to pack and leave. My mother asked him why, and he told her earnestly and anxiously that "the Germans" were coming to get them.

And then it was Monday, September 22. I went to see Daddy in the early afternoon. He was sitting at the kitchen table, slumped over in his seat, eating *muhallabiyyeh*, Middle Eastern milk pudding. He was wearing an orange polo shirt, the very same shirt he had been wearing a few days before when I came to visit him. On that particular evening, I had found Mommy in my bedroom, on the bed, weeping. I'd sat with her silently for a bit, and then I'd gone into the living room. Daddy was dozing on the couch. I'd sat next to him, and he'd woken with a start. "Little *Naj*!" he'd cried. He'd studied my face and seen the sadness. He'd asked me what was wrong. I'd told him nothing was. He'd asked me if it was Rob, my ex-boyfriend. Did I still miss him?

"Do you want me to call him and fix it, Naji? I will! Get me the phone!"

"No, Daddy, it's okay, it's not like calling my teacher when I didn't do my homework. There's nothing to fix."

I'd begun to weep. Daddy had patted his left shoulder, inviting me to put my head there and cry. I did so. He'd then drifted off to sleep again, periodically waking to make sure my head was still on his shoulder, muttering, "I love it. I love it," when he'd been reassured, and then he would doze off again.

Now he was in the kitchen in that same bright orange shirt, hiccuping. He had been hiccuping for fourteen hours or so. Sometimes that happened because of chemo. We didn't know it, but this time it was happening because the tumor in his belly was breaking down. I said hi to Luz, the housekeeper, who was standing at the sink. She looked

up from the dishes and said, "Hi, Mama," very somberly. I
followed her eyes to Daddy. She shook her head. "I don't
know, Mama, it's very bad."

I said hi to Daddy and he said he wanted to go rest. I
took him to the bedroom. He asked me for a blanket. I gave
him one. He said, "*No! A blanket!*" He looked at me pleadingly. He had meant something else. I finally figured out
what (a pair of shorts) and handed it to him. He lay on the
bed and asked me to stay a bit. I told him I had to go to
work soon but I'd stay a bit longer. I asked if he wanted
to drink an Ensure Plus. He liked them now. They were
helping him. They reminded me of being anorexic, and I
felt guilty as I got one from the fridge and poured it into
a glass. I brought it to Daddy and held the straw for him so
he could sip.

"Who's in the tube?" he asked me.

"What?"

"Who's in the tube?"

"What tube, Daddy? I don't understand."

"*Who is in the tube?*" he yelled, pointing at the glass.

"Um. It's Ensure Plus. It's strawberry, like you asked."

He nodded, and fell asleep. It hurt more than anything
to watch him lose his words, his articulacy; the very thing
that had made him who he was. About thirty minutes later,
I got up to leave. He looked at me and said, "Stay a bit, stay
a bit." I said I'd come back after work, or the next day. I

called Mommy and said, "He's not okay. Can't you leave work?" She told me to ask Wadie to come be with him. I called Wadie, who would come after an interview.

I went to work. Wadie went back home and found Daddy in bad shape. He and Mommy took him to the hospital on Long Island that night. We knew that this was the end.

Tutoring a student in the early evening, I told him I thought my father was going to die that night. He asked me why I thought that. I told him the story of the Ensure Plus and how my mom and brother were taking him to the hospital. Ben, my student, all of sixteen years old, said to me, "He was asking you what flavor it was. That's what that means." He knew because he worked with kids who had Down syndrome, and that's how they talked sometimes. Ben then went to his room and brought me a book. It was by Lance Armstrong, and it was about how he survived cancer. "Your dad might be okay. Just keep hoping."

It was the sweetest gesture I could have imagined.

On Tuesday we went to the hospital. Daddy was on lots of drugs. Mommy had to call my uncle Nadim, a doctor in Beirut, to ask if she should agree to put Daddy on a breathing machine. When Nadim heard the question, he began to cry. Then Mommy began to cry, and then I did. We told the doctor to do it, but we knew that once he was on that tube, it meant he was going to die.

When I got back to Manhattan, I met Rob for coffee. My shoe had come undone in the morning, and I hadn't retied it all day. Rob told me my dad would be fine. Rob told me not to cry. Rob told me to get over our relationship. I asked Rob to please check on me the next day. He said he would, but I should really start to move on. I left him at the subway and began to convulse in sobs. Some people on the street tried to call an ambulance for me, but I insisted I was fine, and got in a cab back uptown to my parents' apartment.

Daniel Barenboim, my daddy's best friend, was there. Rashid and Mona, family friends who are more like family, were there. I went to sleep. I hadn't even stopped crying on my pillowcase when Wadie's wife, Jennifer, tapped on the door, and cracked it open. In the sliver of light that entered the room, I saw her silhouette in the doorway. She was clutching the portable phone, almost tenderly. Her hand was shaking; she was crying but trying to pretend she wasn't. I was taken aback by her sniffles, and at once honored that she loved him enough to cry too and worried that she needed to be comforted by someone and that no one would be able to do it because we would all be weeping too. I sat up in bed with a start, anticipating what she was about to say, trying to make my body as strong and still as possible, in a ridiculous attempt to shield my insides from the power of the words she was about to utter.

"Naj," she said quietly, her voice quivering, "uuuum, th-they want us to go to the hospital and, uhhhhh-m, and, uh-hhhm, say good-bye now." Her voice broke on the last word, as if on cue. I thought I tried to stand up right away, but I realized three seconds later that I hadn't moved an inch, and I physically could not get up. The room was spinning. I thought of how I'd often read about things like that happening at moments like this, and mused on how I had never actually believed they occurred in real life. After a few minutes, Mona came into the dark room and lay on the bed with me. She held me, she stroked my hair. The lights from buildings across the river in New Jersey encircled us in an eerie glow that somehow felt safe and protective, while the light streaming in from the hallway—jarring and awful—seemed to beckon menacingly for me to come to it.

Mona finally helped me stand up. As soon as my feet touched the wood floor, my knees buckled. They felt like Jell-O. I looked at Mona, wondering how she had seemed to know that would happen; she hadn't let go of me. Once again, I thought about how I had never believed that that sort of thing happened in real life. My legs wobbled. I almost landed on the floor. This very petite woman was literally pulling me up with all her strength; it was real: I could not stand. Mona slowly guided me toward the blinding corridor light, and though I could barely walk, I felt grateful for the task I had to focus on, simply not falling

down. I was grateful I had something to think about besides my daddy, and I walked into the hall.

☙

DADDY DIDN'T DIE that night though. He lasted one
more day. We spent all of Wednesday in the intensive care
unit of the hospital, watching him, waiting for his last
breath. The inevitability of his death felt like the greatest
weight I had ever borne. I wondered how the ICU nurses
didn't cry, or scream, or act sad as they bustled about, performing their ritual tasks and filling out their charts while
death hung over the room. Lined up in a neat row, connected to myriad machines and monitors, were unconscious,
bedridden people who might die at any moment. One of
them was my father. I thought of *The Sopranos*, and how
people on that show were always getting shot and killed and
how I never cried about it. I felt sad for their families, for
their children. I cried and cried for every person whose life
had been irrevocably altered by the death of a loved one; I
realized I had never cared enough, or understood enough. I
thought of the young man we had seen going for a jog earlier that morning as we climbed into the car; I had given
him a look of such venom and hatred for just going about
his daily business on the day my father was going *to die*.
Now I forgave him, because I had done the same thing

every day of my life, and every day of my life someone somewhere had died and their loved ones had felt the way I was feeling now.

A doctor came into the room. He told us carefully that Daddy was going to die at some point within the next twenty-four hours, adding, "It's just a matter of his last breath."

Dr. Rai came into the room. He had been Daddy's doctor for twelve years. He had become part of our lives, part of our family, really. He had cried the day before; he had tried to hide it, but we had all seen it. He had said something like, "Edward Said, as we knew him, is now gone," and he too had added something about it being a matter of Daddy's last breath, before he briskly left the room so as to not reveal his tears. Now he was here to tell us to "say good-bye and go home." There was no point in just watching Daddy, Dr. Rai said.

He died the next morning, on Thursday, September 25, 2003, at six forty-five a.m., there, in Long Island Jewish Hospital.

Within one day, my entire extended family and most of our friends had descended upon our apartment. They had flown in from Lebanon, Jordan, Europe, California, everywhere. They all stayed with us as long as they were able, some up to two weeks. Francesco arrived from L.A. on Friday morning and didn't leave my side for five days. Jenny called me on Thursday, moments after Daddy was gone. Now a journalist, she knew, she said, because "it was on the wire this morning." It was also already on the front page of *The New York Times*; the Indian lady at the newsstand on the corner had offered us her condolences right away. I sent an e-mail to a group listserve I was on, confirming his passing to the hundreds of people who had been asking if it was true; I just didn't want to keep getting e-mails saying "Edward Said is *dead*." By the end of the day, my e-mail had circled the world countless times and had even made it to the desk of Kofi Annan at the UN. Two thousand people came to the funeral; Susan Sontag was crying; people were staring at her, at Noam Chomsky, at Peter Jennings. Al Jazeera broadcast the funeral. I got *thousands* of e-mails and phone calls. And it was at this point only that I realized what "world famous" meant.

We carried his ashes to Lebanon and buried them in the Quaker family cemetery in Brummana, my mother's ancestral village. It is what he wanted. People, sometimes in outrage, asked why he was not laid to rest in Palestine. These were the people who saw him as a human symbol of a geographical place. These people make me crazy, even though they mean well. It actually never occurred to us to bury Daddy in Palestine, because Palestine, though a cause he embraced wholeheartedly and fought for his entire adult life, is a place he hadn't really known. The world had conflated "Edward Said" with Palestine, but I had not. I had only really ever known Daddy, but how could I explain that to the world?

So I spent nearly a year comforting other people who mourned my father. Almost every time I said "I miss my dad," someone would say, "Oh, we all do," and begin to wax eloquent on how he had changed their life. (To be honest, this still happens every time I say I miss my dad.) It was always qualified, of course, but usually in a way that didn't make me feel better: "He was your real father, but he was a father to us all." I felt I couldn't have my dad to myself. I did not know how to mourn "Edward Said," and I did not want to mourn my daddy.

I spent the following summer in Lebanon, alone. At the end of that summer, I felt as though I had been saved. Something about going back to a place that held me so tightly as a child helped me grieve. From then on, I returned twice a year to be with my dad. More than just feeling lucky to come from a beautiful seaside paradise, I felt overwhelmingly grateful that it had been returned to me, after a childhood of embarrassment, pain, and confusion over "where I am from."

The next summer, whole again and in need of a trip back to really enjoy myself completely, I returned to Beirut, again alone. It was the carefree, happy summer I had longed for as a teenager. I had never, not in a million years, dreamed I would find it there.

We had driven south, to the beach, four of us, young, happy, vibrant. I sat in the backseat of the car and marveled at the scenario:

I, a Lebanese Palestinian American, had been invited to the beach by three of my friends—two American and one British—all of whom lived in Beirut permanently. As the two boys in the front seat argued about the best travel route and competed over their knowledge of the highways of my mother's country, I smiled to myself. Funny that I'm the only person in the car who is Lebanese by blood, I thought, for these three loved and lived in Lebanon with a passion that might, in another place, be expected only from a native.

That perfect day was spent in the sun, on the beautiful beaches near Sidon, and at the end of it, we rented Jet Skis on a whim, and rode out on the waves, laughing as the beautiful sun set behind us on the Mediterranean Sea.

In the car home, I felt wonderful, and I was filled with a sense of wholeness. I blurted out, "My God, this is the most beautiful place on earth, I am so lucky to be from here." My friends agreed. Even more exciting was that my friends in the States were finally ready to accept that the war in Lebanon was a memory; they wanted to come visit, to experience the nightlife, the beaches, the food, the shopping, the generosity of spirit and the warmth of the Lebanese people that I had described in detail, that they had seen in my family. Some were even saving their money for the lavish beach wedding I told them I would have there . . . as soon as I found someone to marry.

I sat quietly in the backseat, all the way to Beirut. I was content to just take in the beauty, the safety, the comfort of the atmosphere, the jasmine-mingled-with-diesel-fuel-and-*za'atar* smell of the streets. Lebanon was really, truly, finally my safe haven, my home, again.

And though I was thirty-one years old, I had my first Lebanon kiss that very same week. It was a whirlwind romance, the kind I had become very good at having since my father's death. It was passionate, intense, bizarre, and very, very short, but it was magical. My last night in town we said good-bye to each other with a mad kiss in the elevator of my grandfather's building, the very same elevator that had been out of service so many times during my childhood because of the lack of electricity, the elevator that had taken me to and from my jiddo's home since I was three weeks old. I had spent my entire adolescence lost and disconnected from Lebanon. I had been in pain and isolation and what felt like torment in America, longing to feel "normal," and now I was having an exquisite carefree summer of irreverence in a place that felt like home. I felt so lucky.

☙

THEN, IN MAY OF 2006, I jetted off for what was to be my third magnificent summer in Lebanon. On Tuesday, July 11, I spent another day at the beach, this time in Tyre, farther south, with a different set of friends. We happily splashed about in the bluest water you can imagine. Floating on top of the sea on my back, I followed my lazy gaze over to the land of Israel, which was just a few miles away. I giggled; this was the first time I was anywhere near the border and not being forced to think about the conflict. I loved my home. I loved that I belonged somewhere. The blueprint was set for another perfect summer.

The next day I learned that in the south, near the border with Israel, Hizbullah had captured some Israeli soldiers. This was a common occurrence there; it happened on both sides and rarely affected life in Beirut, so I didn't think too much of it. But the day got weirder. All of my journalist friends disappeared into their work. Something really "fucked up" was "going on in the south," one of them told me in a text message. I went to bed early, hoping that by the morning everything would be normal again.

I woke at six a.m. to the familiar sound of bombs. The Israeli invasion of 2006 had officially begun. The airport was the first thing to be bombed. I realized I was trapped, and I was alone. My mom was not there to make decisions for me this time, and my Lebanese family members seemed so accustomed to the sounds of war that they weren't exactly helpful. They could tell exactly how far away a bomb was and what kind of bomb it was; I could only hear that it sounded like it was downstairs.

"No, that's an echo over the mountain; it sounds like it's near Sidon," my uncle would say, but I had no idea how he was able to figure that out.

"They're bombing the south; they are completely destroying Tyre; they're not bombing us," an aunt explained. I froze, thinking of the families I had swum near the day before—they must all be either dead, or homeless.

"Oh my God," I shrieked, "but I was *just* there!"

"Well, Naji, it's a good thing you went on Tuesday and not on Wednesday," my uncle joked (this is typical Lebanese humor).

I did not understand how all of my aunts and uncles somehow knew beyond the shadow of a doubt that Beirut was not going to be destroyed. And then the war logic began to emerge:

"You see, Naji, they won't bomb here because there are no Shiites in this neighborhood," my aunt explained.

"And also we are near the American University. We can always go across the street to the campus and be safe because they won't bomb it—that would be the equivalent of bombing America, and the Israelis would *never* do that," another one added.

"Shall we go up to the mountains, where it's all Christians? Maybe you will calm down."

"Well, maybe it's worse if you take her there. There is a power plant up there, and they might bomb the power plant like they're doing in Gaza."

I wanted to scream. The bombs did come closer. All day and all night we were trapped inside, in front of CNN and our computers. The streets were deserted, everything was closed. Israeli drones circled overhead endlessly. I shuddered every time I heard their loud moan.

"If you can hear the plane you are safe; if you don't hear the plane it means it's right on top of you and you are going to die," yet another helpful relative offered.

"Excellent," I declared cynically. "So, not only is the noise of the drone harrowing in itself, but every time it falls silent, there is no relief? You have to worry about whether you are about to be killed by the silence? Who invented this?"

There's something I want to explain. And I want to be clear about it. You can spend your life being a humanist, a pacifist, a thoughtful person who does not even think about hating, or does not even know what it *is* to hate—that is to say, you can really and truly be a human being who is tolerant and open-minded and humane, judging people by how they behave toward you, and treating them the way you wish to be treated, *but* when you are being attacked, when bombs are falling around you, planes are hovering over your head, when your life is in danger and you are scared, it is *so easy* to look up to the sky and feel abject, boiling hatred for the people doing this to you, and curse them out.

When you are fearful for your life, and you are being bombed by a certain group of people, you are not thinking, *Oh, but I know that not all Israelis agree with this.* There is no time for that. Just as there is no time for *them* to think that it is not all Lebanese attacking back. And there is no time to think about the Israeli pilot who wishes he weren't in the plane dropping bombs on everybody. All you can think in these situations is, *Fuck everyone!* The summer of 2006 was the first time I had ever experienced real, pure, true hate.

But it was fleeting; it passed. I calmed down and I rationalized. But that was because of a few things: (1) I was able to get *out*; (2) I am lucky enough to know some good people on the "other side"; and (3) I was able to talk on the phone daily with my Jewish therapist in New York. So imagine if you grow up trapped in a conflict region, and you are always fearful, and you are under constant threat of attack. Whether you are an Israeli or an Arab, you are going to continue to *hate* unless you have an alternative. And many people don't.

Five days later, I was able to get on a Spanish convoy out

of the country, with the help of my father's (Israeli) best friend. After a twenty-hour bus trip to Damascus (normally a trip of two hours), and a three-day stay there with Maha's parents, I flew to London, and then finally, home.

∞

THOUGH I HAVE NEVER returned to Palestine, Palestine always returns to me. In May of 2007 I went back to Lebanon. On a car ride to a beach party in the south, I learn that something is happening in the north, in a Palestinian refugee camp. I know about these refugees. They have been here, for forty years, sixty years, now four hundred thousand of them, in camps that were supposed to be temporary homes. Although when they arrived they were welcomed with sympathy, now they are clearly resented. Accordingly, they can't have anything more than a menial job in Lebanon proper, only in the camps, where the conditions are squalid, and many live on UN handouts. Many of them were born here. They have never known and will probably never know Palestine. But they will never really know Lebanon either. They cannot be Lebanese citizens because they are Palestinian.

Some strange militant Islamic group has infiltrated the camp. The militants are apparently not Palestinian, they are from all over—Tunisia, Afghanistan, Pakistan—they are an "offshoot of Al Qaeda . . ." but, as Wadie explains on the phone later, "*Naj*—the Palestinians are a soft target—they have no power in Lebanon so they can easily be manipulated."

At a party that night, I hear some Lebanese people say awful things about Palestinians. Despite the fact that my mom is one hundred percent Lebanese and my dad one quarter, I will never be given a Lebanese passport (you can't pass citizenship to your children if you are a woman).

But in Lebanon, am I not really a Palestinian either, because I am not "one of those people" in the camps? Because I have a U.S. passport and a famous father? Because I am a Christian? I hate that the Palestinians in the camps are becoming refugees *again*, and I am drinking wine on a balcony.

And yet in America, there is no doubt that since 9/11, I am officially an Arab, bridging the gap between two worlds that don't understand each other.

&

ONE SUNDAY I go to Zabar's to get some food, to waste time, and as I'm walking up Broadway I see two young women coming toward me: one is wearing a "Free Palestine" T-shirt and the other has a piece of paper taped to her shirt saying something about Palestinians. Then all of a sudden there's a whole group of them, with these weird photocopied pages taped to their chests, and I'm thinking, *What a cheap-looking protest sign.* And so the whole bunch of them come at me, one after the other, after the other (but really there are only about ten), and I'm thinking, *Where's the protest?* and *How come the white people always know about them and I never do?* and I'm thinking that I'm jealous of the girl's "Free Palestine" T-shirt because it's the one I'd want: black, plain, simple, small, and fitted; cute, really. And I'm thinking that I should stop and buy one. But all the while, I have these intense chills, the chills I get when I hear the word "Palestine" spoken aloud, and I feel immensely grateful that these people are protesting for me, my people, my cause. And so I really want to jump in, find the end of the line, cry, hug them, and be a revolutionary. And when I pass the guy whose eight-and-a-half-by-eleven says "Palestinians are human beings," I almost lose it and really do start crying, my chills are so intense . . . because I am this girl, this young woman, this whatever, this . . . *me*, I am this *Palestinian*—walking by them all with my mouth slightly open because I want to do, say, give, think *something*. And I'm thinking how I can't; and that I shouldn't, and what *would* I do, say? And I'm thinking that Palestinians *are* human beings and isn't it ironic that here comes one now, walking down the street? But what am I supposed to do when people are protesting *for* me, and how am I supposed to react when people who are about as far removed from the plight of Palestinians as anyone could ever possibly be are walking down the street, talking about my people's suffering, a suffering I still don't even fully understand? And I'm thinking that words are so powerful, because "Palestine," that word, makes me want to cry.

೧

IN THE LAST DECADE I have been invited to speak, talk, write, and create theater as an "Arab-American." I have felt my love and happiness and connection to the Middle East grow; I have fallen in love with Lebanon and am as happy and comfortable there as I am here. I have learned to speak up about the truth of what I have seen. But *none* of that has made me less of an Upper West Side princess. None of it changes the fact that I started and finished school in America, that English is my first language, that I still live in New York. None of it.

೧

WITH A GREAT DEAL of outside encouragement and support, in 2009 I turned my life story into a play, and the play has now evolved into this book. I performed the play

Off Broadway for two months, and I continue to perform it all over the country, mainly at high schools and colleges, which I love.

I needed to be coaxed into writing my story because I still have a lot of insecurities about my abilities, my intelligence, and my authority to speak about the problems in the Middle East. I worried I didn't know enough about my dad's work, I was scared of making political statements of any kind, I was afraid of sounding like a whining spoiled brat, and, most important, I felt that whatever I wrote would not be helpful or educational for Americans, since I myself had more questions to ask than answers to give. But as I began writing, the stories came easily, and they were funny even when they were sad. And when I began performing, I realized people were willing to listen, because it was simply my story, and *precisely because* it was sort of messy and embarrassing and atypical, yet also universal in its complexity; having a mixed-up identity actually makes it easier to relate to a larger and more varied group of people. In addition, being able to laugh at my younger self and point out how much I *didn't* care about anything serious as a teenager (and still sometimes don't) allowed people to learn along with me, and rest easy in their confusion and varying degrees of perplexity and apathy over the problems in the Middle East.

And even though I have gotten far more standing ovations than I have ever gotten boos (I've gotten boos exactly once, in exactly one place in the script, when I read just an excerpt, out of context), every single time I perform the play, I am petrified of being hated, ridiculed, misunderstood, belittled, and heckled. High schools are particularly terrifying, for many of the same reasons that they are when you're a student in high school, but also because they all vary so greatly depending on the community they are in—the socioeconomic class of the students, their age, religion, and gender. Also, high school students are more likely to be forced to sit through a performance at an assembly, whereas college students tend to make the decision to come and see it because of a personal interest in theater, or the Middle East, or my father's scholarship. Since the Internet has made the entire world instantly accessible and information readily available, since 9/11 occurred and the Iraq and Afghanistan wars followed, college campuses are also filled with students who read and think about and study the Middle East critically, and do not easily accept the stereotypes and images they are fed by the mainstream media. (Thanks in part to my dad's scholarly contributions. I can't lie!)

The most profound experiences have been at high schools in New York City, my hometown. The first time I performed at one, a young woman wrote a paper about the experience of seeing me, confessed to her own eating disorder, and asked her parents and teachers for help. I was beyond moved. My show has since had the same effect on a few other young New York City high school students, one of whom has Palestinian parents. Her mother called one day to thank me for "saving my daughter's life." Those instances, in which I have actually helped someone stay alive, are rare, and though they touch me deeply, I am glad they do not happen too often. What I do love, though, is being reminded each time I visit a school, just how powerful honesty can be. I tell my stories, I make fun of my flaws, I loudly proclaim my embarrassment and bring my family's struggles to life on stage again and again, and through this, I somehow manage to make these students feel less alone in all of their complexity and awkwardness, at the exact age when they are going to start to have to confront their own identities.

About a year and a half ago, I did my play for the students at a coed private school in Manhattan. It was a school much like Trinity, but different in that it has always had a much more Jewish student body (the faculty actually had to screen my performance first, at the request of the parents, who wanted to make sure it wasn't controversial). The students loved it, but as is always the case when I perform, I didn't really understand the full depth of my effect on the kids until I chatted with a group of them in the lunchroom afterward. One girl asked me how she should talk to her Jewish grandmother, who had once gone so far as to accuse her of being "anti-Semitic" when she said something that was critical of the Israeli government; another girl told me that she felt most at home in a country that she'd recently visited but to which she had no familial or ancestral ties. "Here, though, in New York, I'm just like everyone else; I'm a white person. A Jewish person."

Two girls came toward me at the end. One asked if I remembered her. Within an instant I smiled and rushed to hug her. I had tutored her when she was eleven. Now she was a senior in high school. I remembered her as a sassy, smart (she might as well have tutored me), and hilarious little girl, who charmed me the minute I shook her hand and said my name.

"Your name is *Nejla*," she had said, correcting the American pronunciation I had automatically used. "That name is Turkish."

"Yes." I'd smiled. "It's Arabic. And you're right; it is pronounced *Nejla*."

She looked at me as if I had eight heads and said, challengingly, "Then why'd you say it wrong?"

When I learned her parents were Turkish but also Jewish, I remember thinking, *Oh well, that's why she has more confidence than I did at that age. She's Jewish, so she fits in.*

Now she stood in front of me, almost a woman, thanking me for articulating for her so much of what she felt inside. I just hugged her repeatedly and said "yay" about eight hundred times, because I didn't know what else to say or do.

A few weeks later she sent me her college-application essay, which my performance had inspired her to rewrite entirely, just before it was due.

I wish I could describe myself to you [she'd written]. *How I work. I am Deborah, Debosh, Deboosh, and Debooshka, born a Turk in America; a Sephardic Jew from a Muslim country; bat mitzvahed in an Ashkenazi temple on the Upper West Side; a Mediterranean, classified as Middle Eastern; able to identify with all of it, and with none. I am other and I am not alone. Somewhere in all of us there is that same thing that I share with Najla, that otherness where our stories truly begin, that otherness that makes us belong.*

I just cried. I finally felt like I had a place on this earth.

ACKNOWLEDGMENTS

Heaps of gratitude to Sarah McGrath and Sarah Stein at Riverhead; Jin Auh, Jackie Ko, Mariam Said, Wadie Said and Jennifer Zacharia, Grace Said, Mona Damluji (Junior), Rob Quatrone, Sturgis Warner, Lou Moreno, Francesco Luparello, Tala Manassah, Beth Althofer, Jim Nicola, Linda Chapman, Maha Chehlaoui, Leila Buck, Danae Elon, Omar Metwally, Omar Koury, James Asher, Afaf Shawwa, Sarah Gardner Borden, Hani Omar Khalil, Denise Burrell-Stinson, Jenny Badner Falcon, Hind Shoufani, Deborah Altaras, and my absolutely favorite nephew, Edward, just because.

Najla Said has performed Off Broadway, regionally and internationally, as well as in film and television. In April 2010, Najla completed a nine-week sold-out Off Broadway run of her solo show, *Palestine*, which features some of the material in this book. She lives in New York City.